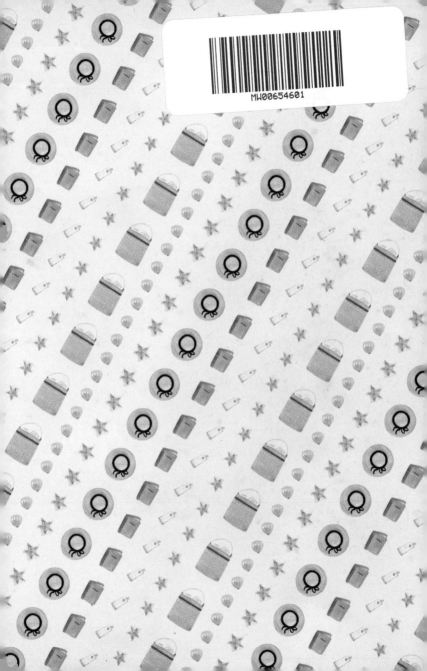

MW00654601

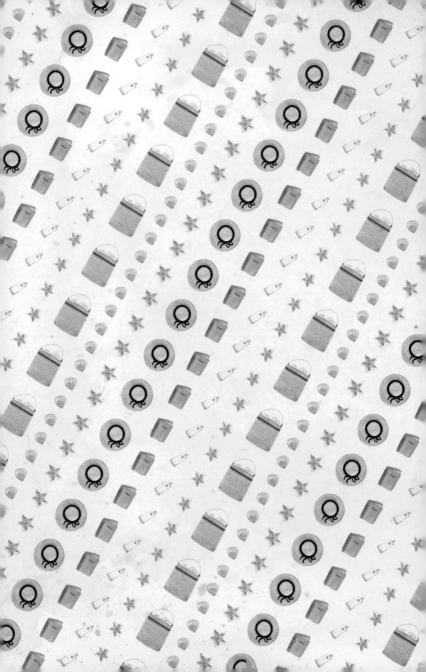

To

_____

From

_____

Date

_____

The BEACH is Calling

90 DEVOTIONS FOR REST AND RELAXATION

DaySpring

LIVE YOUR FAITH

The Beach is Calling: 90 Devotions for Rest and Relaxation
Copyright © 2021 DaySpring Cards, Inc. All rights reserved.
First Edition, May 2021

Published by:

21154 Highway 16 East
Siloam Springs, AR 72761
dayspring.com

Written by: Bonnie Rickner Jensen
Cover Design by: Jessica Wei
Illustrations by: Stephanie Henry

Printed in China
Prime: J4966
ISBN: 978-1-64454-985-8

CONTENTS

TRUE REST

Truly my soul finds rest in God.

PSALM 62:1 NIV

Ocean and horizon are like trust and rest. Inseparable. If we don't learn to trust God, we won't experience true rest. Rest is a constant craving of our hearts, in the moments of our hardest days, in the weeks of our longest waits, in the months that bring more questions than answers. Physical rest is planned but spiritual rest is priority. When we trust God, we are teaching our souls to rest in Him no matter what happens. He's *here* and He *sees*. What we need. Where we're going. When is best. In the same way there's a steady, refreshing breeze at the ocean's edge, there's a steadfast, reassuring purpose at the heart of God's plan for our lives. Trust and rest come by believing His plans for us are always driven by perfect love.

How do we keep our face toward our purpose and the love guiding it? We keep our focus on hope as ceaseless as the waves. We keep our confidence in faithfulness as sure as the sunrise. We keep our prayers grateful for God's goodness and honest for our growth. He knows us and sees us with cloudless clarity. That should inspire us to trust Him with

fearless courage. When we move through our days brave and hopeful, our souls find rest in a world that's fighting to reel our minds and spirits in the opposite direction. Trusting God is the divine tug that will win us the battle.

Today is another chance to remind ourselves that we need to give it all to God—the pain, the why-did-this-happen, the humanness of our doubt, the reality of our fears. He'll take it all in one fell swoop of love, leaving in its place a lighter spirit, a brighter hope, and a deeper trust. The rest that follows will be like sunshine to our souls and as soothing as sand between our toes.

FATHER, I TRUST YOU WITH
MY CARES, MY DAY, AND MY JOURNEY.
EVERY HOPE I HAVE IS IN YOUR PERFECT LOVE,
THE ONLY PLACE MY SOUL FINDS PERFECT REST.

A TIME TO SIT AND THINK

Relax, everything's going to be all right; rest, everything's coming together; open your hearts, love is on the way!

JUDE 1-2 THE MESSAGE

The only way to plop down in our beach chair, dig our feet into the sand, look out over the turquoise water, and breathe in the salty air—*spiritually* speaking—is to believe beyond any shadow of every doubt that love is leading us. God's best is always grounded in love and it's always what He wants for our lives: the *best* next step; the *best* path to our growth; the *best* outcome. We all have days when the waves crash relentlessly and our beach bag, filled with everything we thought we needed, goes floating out to sea. We sit silent, soaking wet, and feeling helpless. Those are the days when the deeper breaths are needed, the fearless faith is tested, and the blind trust that everything is coming together for our good is more important than the overwhelming circumstances in front of us. Especially when it looks like the circumstances have washed away all our hopes and dreams.

Our days come one at a time and grace sufficient to handle each 24-hour increment comes too, without fail. We have what we need when we need it. Every day will not be a day at the beach physically *or* spiritually. But every day *will* move us toward a place where we exercise more trust, enjoy more peace, and look a little more like Jesus. That's all that really matters because that's all that's eternally measured—what we do to point others to *Him*.

Some things we pack in our "survival" bags from day-to-day weigh us down and slow our progress. God allows the washing away of dependencies we hold too tightly, self-security we lean on too much, and material things distracting us too often. He wants us to rest in Him just like we relax into a day at the beach. A time to sit and think about the magnitude of His love, the never-ending waves of His grace, and His thoughts of us that *outnumber* the grains of sand. He doesn't rest while caring for every detail of our lives. That frees us to rest in knowing *everything's* coming together for good—with an ocean of love behind it.

FATHER, I'M RELAXED
IN YOUR LOVING CARE TODAY.

WHO ELSE?

Who else has held the oceans
in his hands?

ISAIAH 40:12 TLB

Who else holds the pages of your life in his hands? Who else holds the hope of your days in his hands? Who else holds you, and everything you need, in his hands? The magnitude and fullness of God is more than our minds can comprehend. But I believe our hearts can perceive it in the things He created. Very often I see people standing on the beach at the water's edge, still and gazing outward. The ocean is magnificent. God has held it in His hands. The magnitude and fullness of who He is has a piercing effect here.

On days that feel overwhelming, the ocean is a perfect reminder that the things we worry about are underwhelming against God's presence and promise: "I have made you and I will carry you; I will sustain you and I will rescue you" (ISAIAH 46:4 NIV). There's nothing that can keep Him from coming to our rescue. There's nothing in this world that can stop Him from carrying us when our strength is spent. Even when we don't have an ounce of fight left in us, He won't turn away.

He can't. We are His. *Our names are engraved on the palms of His hands.*

Our rushed lives make it easy to forget how taken care of we are. We have routines, to-do's, obligations, and unexpected challenges that *disrupt* all of the daily things. The weight comes when we let the duties or disruptions distract us from the truth. It takes one second to move our thoughts from the problem to the presence of the One who will give us what we need to solve or survive it. *Pray continually.* For wisdom. For patience. For pause to think about the promise that can't fail. *"I will sustain you."* Rest isn't a thing we pencil in on our calendars, it's a mindset we learn to *live.* I'm not in this alone. God knew this was coming. I have everything I need to handle this because my strength is in Him, and He's held the oceans in His hands.

FATHER, THANK YOU FOR RESETTING MY HEART
TO REST BY REMINDING ME TO CHOOSE
THE *YOU'VE-GOT-ME* SO *WE'VE-GOT-THIS*
MINDSET TODAY.

LISTENING

If I ride the morning winds to the farthest oceans, even there Your hand will guide me.

PSALM 139:9-10 TLB

Oh, the days we feel like escaping. To somehow put our responsibilities, routines, and challenges on hold. Even if it was possible to do, if everything around us stopped and became quiet and uninterrupted, the gentle whisper of the One who loves us most would be there: *"I'm with you. I'm guiding you. I'm paying attention to every detail of your life."* There isn't a place on earth or a space in our being that escapes God's presence. The peace we need and the rest we seek is found in it. Our hope depends on it. Our lives make a difference because of it.

The beach invites us to spend time in the fulness of His presence. There's something about the ocean, salty air, and sand that lulls us into the quiet, uninterrupted parts of ourselves where we're able to listen to His voice. That's how He guides us. His direction isn't audible in chaos, noise, and busyness. His voice is clearest in calmness. Our responsibility is to take the time to get away to our "beach-like" oasis. If the beach isn't possible, maybe a walk, a run, or a solo drive. Or a simple closed door to have a little time to ourselves. We need it because we need Him, and our spiritual health and growth depend on it.

We can keep plowing through our days and praying as we go because we know He's listening, He loves us, and He's there. And praying as we go is a *good* thing. But getting quiet puts us into a better place mentally and spiritually. If we don't make time to hear the other side of the conversations we're having with God, we're missing out on the rest and restoration our spirits need. We're not giving Him our full attention, though we know we have His no matter where we are or what we're doing. We're His priority and that's amazing to think about, but when we make Him *our* priority, we don't have to think about anything. He reminds us again that He's *everything*.

FATHER, I'M QUIET AND LISTENING.
RENEW A RESTFUL SPIRIT IN ME AND
HELP ME HEAR MORE CLEARLY FROM YOU.
THANK YOU FOR ALWAYS BEING THERE.

GRACE-MINDED

*A peaceful heart leads
to a healthy body.*

PROVERBS 14:30 NLT

God isn't concerned about a portion of our well-being; He cares about *all* of it. He's a God of wholeness and healing. He knows the world we live in is a stressful place and the peace He gives is the only way we're getting through it in a healthy, hopeful way. We're human. We're not going to do this perfectly. But we can make a habit of surrendering our days to the one who *did*. Jesus, being one with our unfailing God, allowed no room for doubt. Because of Him we now have the one thing we need to move into the same intimate and confident relationship—grace.

God sees us through the filter of the cross and staying mindful of that is the way to a peaceful heart. Our lives are increasingly bombarded with temptations to be afraid, stressed-out, worried, and anxious. Grace is the antidote. Trust activates it. Love increases its potency. We can do this! God is acquainted with our wiring because He designed it. Knowing how difficult our days would become He provided

a simple remedy—"Trust in the Lord with all your heart" (PROVERBS 3:5 NIV). Our hearts are at the heart of it all. It's ground zero for everything that matters and everything that makes us healthy both physically and spiritually. God is constantly at work there because He knows if the heart is at peace, the mind and body will follow. That's why a *peaceful* heart leads to a *healthy* body. "The Lord does not look at the things people look at. People look at the outward appearance, but the Lord looks at the heart" (I SAMUEL 16:7 NIV).

Trusting in the promises He's given brings the peace we need.

No harm will overtake you. PSALM 91:10 NIV

Never will I leave you; never will I forsake you.
HEBREWS 13:5 NIV

I have made you and I will carry you. ISAIAH 46:4 NIV

I am your shield, your very great reward.
GENESIS 15:1 NIV

His unfailing promises go on and on... Let's go on trusting them with *all* of our heart.

FATHER, "YOU GO BEFORE ME AND FOLLOW ME.
YOU PLACE YOUR HAND OF BLESSING ON MY
HEAD" (PSALM 139:5 NLT). FILL MY HEART WITH
PEACE AND MY BODY WITH HEALTH. GIVE ME THE
CONFIDENCE TO TRUST YOU FEARLESSLY TODAY.

PRESENT IN HIS PRESENCE

I'm in the very presence of God—oh, how refreshing it is!

PSALM 73:27 THE MESSAGE

Some of the traits of a person referred to as a "beach bum" are chill, laid back, calm, and carefree. That sounds like a wonderful way to be and a lot like God wants us to be! While we can't stay in that mode all of the time, we *can* reset our spirit to a place of quietness, stillness, and rest by spending time with Him. He's everywhere and always present, but we're often too busy to be still, enjoy it, and be refreshed by it. Thinking about the beach is not the same as being at the beach—and knowing God is with us is not the same as spending time with Him. It takes silencing distractions, getting alone, and welcoming Him into our innermost thoughts.

There are many different "meeting" places to choose from. Music. Nature. Long walks. Oceanside. Silent prayers before opening your eyes in the morning or when you close them at night. Being present to spend time in God's presence doesn't have to be rigid and scheduled. Impromptu moments can become the most refreshing parts of our day. The important thing is learning that being still and being spiritually quiet can happen anywhere at any time. Are we taking every opportunity, no matter how brief, to be refreshed? God loves to be the reason our hearts and minds take a respite from the chaos of this world.

We can create habits that become havens for us spiritually. Often we give more energy to our physical well-being, but that isn't the most vital use of our resources. "Physical training is of some value, but godliness has value for all things, holding promise for both the present life and the life to come" (1 TIMOTHY 4:8 NIV). Spending time with God renews our soul-strength and sharpens our reflection of Him. We'll start to embody the things that last beyond this life—love, patience, kindness, compassion, and hope. Our time of refreshing can lead to a life so bright with God's likeness that we become the refreshing *others* need, and the light that points searching hearts to Him.

FATHER, HELP ME BE MINDFUL
OF SPENDING TIME IN YOUR PRESENCE,
SO I'LL BE REFRESHED AND READY TO BE LIKE YOU.

CALMING THE STORM

*He quiets the raging oceans
and all the world's clamor.*

PSALM 65:7 TLB

There will be noisy days. Not in sound, but in our minds. The list of things we need to do, the immediate things clamoring for our attention, the feeling of uncertainty about what's ahead. Our thought-life can seem like a raging ocean at times. How do we quiet it? How do we create enough calm to hear and know God's wisdom and direction, and to keep our flesh in check? We trust that if He can quiet a raging ocean and a perilous storm on a lake by speaking to them, His words can also quiet our minds. Relax, take a deep breath, and speak to the mental "storms."

> *Lord, when doubts fill my mind, when my heart is in turmoil, quiet me and give me renewed hope and cheer.* PSALM 94:19 TLB

> *A calm, cool spirit keeps the peace.*
> PROVERBS 15:18 THE MESSAGE

> *God has not given us a spirit of fear, but of power and of love and of a sound mind.* II TIMOTHY 1:7 NKJV

We have the words. We have the choice to use them. And God has the power to back them! Every time the noise of this world tries to drown out the words He's given us, we have to mentally grab hold of them again—as many times a day as needed and as often as the doubts come. His words are the only thing that can truly quiet our minds. They're the life preserver that's *always* within reach. Even when we break down and our day feels unmanageable, our goals seem unreachable, and life feels unbearably out of control, the right words can give us strength to stand and keep standing. Once we speak truth and remind ourselves again that God can be trusted, we get braver in the face of our storms. They will not overtake us because God cannot fail. And the wind and the waves never forget Who rules them.

FATHER, THANK YOU FOR GIVING ME
THE WORDS TO QUIET MY MIND AND
KEEP MY SPIRIT CALM AND CONFIDENT IN YOU.

BOUNDARY OF LOVE

He assigned the sea its boundaries and locked the oceans in vast reservoirs.

PSALM 33:7 NLT

The view of the ocean from a beach chair is one of the most enjoyed, sought-after views in the world. Maybe it's because the ocean displays the power of God and the magnitude of His grace at the same time. Its waters could leave their boundaries and overtake the earth, but they never will because His mercy is *overwhelmingly* good. His compassions are new every morning when the sun breaks the horizon. The ocean is a powerful reminder of the depth of God's love, the glory of His creation, and the faithfulness of every promise He's made.

The ocean also has a way of heightening our sense of reverence. We feel small and humbled in the face of it, while reflecting on the One who locked it in its vast reservoir and drew its boundary. Thankfully, our feeling small has nothing to do with the infinite value He put on us, proven by what

He *did* for us. His are the actions of a love deeper and wider than all the oceans on earth combined. How is it that we let ourselves think, for even a moment, that God hasn't put our lives in the perfect place at the perfect time? How can we question the boundary He puts around our days with the promise: *"Nothing crosses into this life without going through the filter of My eternal love for them"*?

"The Lord's unfailing love surrounds the one who trusts in Him" (PSALM 32:10 NIV). Trusting God means that His unfailing love surrounds everything that happens in our lives. He can be trusted to do what's best, with a heart that's best, for the best, most loving outcome. What a beautiful, *boundless* hope that is for us. When we're tempted to doubt or ask why, we need to paint a mental picture of sitting on the beach looking out over the ocean, and remind ourselves again that the One who holds it in place also holds us—and He won't let *either* out of the palm of His hand.

FATHER, I TRUST YOU!
MY COMFORT AND HOPE IS KNOWING THAT
EVERYTHING IN MY DAY IS SURROUNDED
BY LOVE THAT WILL NEVER FAIL.

HOPE STRONG

*You are the only hope...
throughout the world and far
away upon the sea.*

PSALM 65:5 TLB

*H*ope. It sounds like a good place to unfold our chairs and rest our weary souls in today—if only for a few beach-like moments! Hope, as with so many worthwhile things, takes some nurturing on our part. It can suffer from complaining, doubting, and neglecting to renew our minds to the truth of what God says. Hope can also get crowded out by circumstances that don't improve as quickly as we'd like them to or believe they should. We're human, impatient, and we like to see results.

God knows that for hope to sustain us for the greater things He has for our lives, it's going to need some strengthening. Some core strengthening. In the process of battling through doubt, quieting our complaining, and going back to His Word to train our minds to hold onto truth, hope learns to thrive. And when hope thrives, there's less that can bring us down.

There aren't as many trials that can keep us in bed all day. There are fewer storms that scare us, and far more that we can sail through with a smile on our face and joy in our spirit.

Hope is caring for ourselves enough to believe God stands at the frontline of every battle leading us to the win. Through Him, we win. We can believe in us because we can trust in Him. We can only be confident and secure and sure because He is our hope. We can do life bravely and boldly because He loves us beyond measure, beyond our mistakes, and beyond our weaknesses.

Let's care for the hope in our souls today by keeping our minds on Him and our focus on the truth. Before we know it, the hope we carry will be so tough to defeat that we'll begin to believe *anything* is possible—because with God, *it is*.

FATHER, STRENGTHEN MY HOPE
AND READY MY SOUL FOR EVERY PURPOSE
YOU'VE WRITTEN FOR MY LIFE.

Let's start by taking a smallish nap or two.

—WINNIE THE POOH

LITTLE PONDERINGS

I'll ponder all the things You've
accomplished, and give a long,
loving look at Your acts.

PSALM 77:12 THE MESSAGE

One of the best ways to reset our spirit to "joy" and restore our hope to "full" is to meditate on the things God has done in our lives. To think long and thankfully about how He always comes through for us in His perfect timing, the person who spoke just the right words at just the right time, and the parking spot that opened up with perfect timing when we were running late. The little acts of love are often the sweetest because they're glimpses of how present God is every day and in all situations. Daily stresses create the most clutter in our minds. When it comes to clearing the space we need to reflect, reflection takes intentional thought directing. But it can start with one memory that brings a smile and a sense of relief. *Yes!* God did that for me—and He'll do it again! He's faithful and I can trust Him completely.

In the hectic pace of life we sometimes forget how

incredibly thoughtful God is. He pays attention to detail. We believe He's there for the big stuff that happens in our lives but too busy for the rest. We think the mundane is lost in the mix of the much larger things going on in this world. But God is never too busy to be who He says He is in our lives. He's first and foremost our loving Father. And His heart is big enough to handle the pressing worries and concerns we have, along with the seemingly little ones.

Maybe He mentioned ants and mustard seeds to open our eyes to the powerful messages that come in small things. As the script of our life plays out, He wants us to keep seeing and remembering the little love notes He sends. He wants us to keep pondering the miracles too—because He's going to continue sending them. He's here for it all, He's faithful through it all, and He's praiseworthy because of it all. We just need to take a little time to give a long, loving look at the track record of His goodness.

FATHER, KEEP ME KEENLY AWARE OF
YOUR CONSTANT PRESENCE AND
ALL THE WAYS YOU SHOW ME
YOUR LOVE EVERY DAY.

CLEARING THE PATH TO QUIET

Quiet down before God,
be prayerful before Him.

PSALM 37:7 THE MESSAGE

When we're encouraged to quiet down before God and be prayerful, there's a good chance it isn't our voices we need to silence, but our minds. That's where the trouble starts as far as worry, anxiety, and fear go. Thoughts send chain reactions through our bodies, and they're going to be good or bad ones. That's why Paul said to "fix your thoughts on what is true and good and right. Think about things that are pure and lovely" (PHILIPPIANS 4:8 TLB). Paul understood the mind-body connection and he knew our worries and fears could cause us to fold under pressure. If we start to believe things contrary to God's love and truth, anxiety can establish a pathway to destroy our overall well-being.

Getting our minds to quiet down before God begins with filling them up with what His Word says: "Truly my soul finds rest in God" (PSALM 62:1 NIV); "Return to your rest, my soul,

for the Lord has been good to you" (PSALM 116:7 NIV); "Come to Me, all you who are weary and burdened, and I will give you rest" (MATTHEW 11:28 NIV). If the thoughts clamoring for our attention don't come from love and truth, they have to go! Rooting out negativity will get us to a place of relaxing in God's faithfulness. The quicker we pluck out the lies, the faster the quiet comes and the sooner we get to the second part of Psalm 37:7, "be prayerful before Him." Prayer brings the *best* rest to every part of us.

In prayer, we have God's ear, and we learn His heart. It's a conversation that invites us to tap into our *lifeline*. He has time for us no matter what, He's listening to us no matter when, and He forgives and strengthens us no matter how many times we come to the throne of His amazing grace (HEBREWS 4:16). We can *never* exhaust His mercy. And isn't that a beautiful truth to give our spirit, soul, and body the rest it needs today?

FATHER, GIVE ME STRENGTH AND WISDOM
TO PULL THE NEGATIVE "WEEDS" IN MY MIND,
CLEARING THE PATH FOR PEACE, REST,
AND A RENEWED CONFIDENCE IN YOU.

JUST KEEP SURRENDERING

You rule over the surging sea;
when its waves mount up,
You still them.

PSALM 89:9 NIV

Some days it seems God would have an easier time calming the waves of a raging sea than He would getting us to be still and know *He's got us*. Hard days happen and they feel longer when we're fretting. Resting in His care can succumb to fear if we fix our eyes on the list of things going wrong—the car that won't run, the job that isn't there, the budget that looks impossible to meet. These are not unusual troubles in this world, and we aren't alone when we face them. God knew they were coming, and He knows how we're getting through them.

The waters of life will be calm again. The faith-building storm will pass. God is the same at the beginning, middle, and end of each one, but we are *changed*. "Consider it pure joy...whenever you face trials of many kinds" (JAMES 1:2 NIV). How can we rejoice every time it feels like the wind and waves are relentless? When it feels like we're flailing and there's no land or lifeboat in sight? We trust God and the *why* of the trials: "Because you know that the testing of your faith produces perseverance. Let perseverance finish its work so that you may be mature and complete, not lacking anything" (JAMES 1:3-4 NIV).

Complete and lacking nothing comes by completely surrendering to God. I like to think of a popular animated character's encouragement, "Just keep swimming, just keep swimming." Only I change the dialogue a little. "Just keep surrendering, just keep surrendering." Oh, how we want our way, our timing, and our tantrums. It's tough to keep giving everything to God. Can't we hold onto a few things—a little self-pity, a little wanting-our-own-way, a little forcing the outcome to what we think is best?

God is incredibly patient with us. He will *never* give up on us. If we could grasp the magnitude of His love, we'd run to Him with both hands in the air, our hearts open wide, and our souls crying, "Surrender!" and we might suddenly realize we're walking on water right through the storm.

FATHER, SURRENDERING EVERYTHING
TO YOU MEANS LACKING NOTHING I NEED
TO BE COMPLETE. I GIVE MY DAY AND
ALL THAT'S IN IT TO YOU.

A BLANKET OF PEACE

Don't you know He enjoys giving rest to those He loves?

PSALM 127:2 THE MESSAGE

Salty air. Warm sand. Pelicans gliding. Sandpipers scurrying. Saltwater mist. Sun. Soothing shelter from puffy clouds slowly passing. Standing in the surf. Steadying ourselves when the waves pull, and we sink a little as the sand races out from under our feet. Smiling into the face of endless blue water. Everything about being at the beach calls our souls to relax. *And God loves to see it.* We can almost hear Him whisper, "Rest. I have you in the palm of My hand."

As fun as a day at the beach is for us, it's even more enjoyable for our heavenly Father to see us in a relaxed, carefree state of mind. When our hearts and minds are at rest, peace follows. And when we're at peace we're in a place of trust. It makes God happy to be trusted with everything in our lives. Our bodies weren't designed to carry stress. Sadly, burdens can be like blankets for our souls, giving us a false sense of security. We wrap them around us, and it feels comfortable—to be in control, to prove we're capable, to feel

responsible for taking care of everything that concerns us. We carry our cares around until they're all worked out, never mind what the stress is doing to us in the process. It just seems easier to pick up that blanket and drag it along, carrying all the stuff ahead that needs to be resolved, fixed, decided, done, and provided for, even when there isn't a thing we can do about them right now.

Here's where real comfort comes from: "Give your burdens to the Lord. He will carry them. He will not permit the godly to slip or fall" (PSALM 55:22 TLB). Today, let's stop grabbing our "security blankets" of worry and instead spread out our beach blankets of peace. That's when we can fully enjoy God's company by believing He will *never* let us down.

FATHER, YOU ENJOY GIVING ME REST
SO I'M GIVING MY CARES TO YOU.
I TRUST YOUR STRENGTH,
YOUR PLANS FOR ME, AND YOUR LOVE.

THE COMPANY
TO KEEP

Keep company with Me
and you'll learn to live
freely and lightly.

MATTHEW 11:30 THE MESSAGE

What an invitation! We can live freely and lightly without being confined by fear or weighed down by the cares of this world. How do we learn to live with such fearless freedom? By hanging out with God! Our time with Him can be as casual as having coffee with a friend or walking on the beach. And shouldn't it feel that comfortable because we do it so often and know Him so well?

Do you have a set time every day when you pray, praise, give thanks, ask questions, seek answers, and soak in His beautiful, refreshing presence? How would your life change if you woke up each morning to a conversation with God? What would it be like to develop the habit of connecting with God all day long? Of course, there are times when it's necessary to get away from all distractions to pray and listen, but we also need His continual counsel. We need to be mindful of His presence and the comfort it brings.

"Rejoice always, pray continually, give thanks in all circumstances" (I THESSALONIANS 5:16-18 NIV). That sounds like another invitation to keep company with God, which simply means staying tuned-in and aware that He always looks forward to spending time with us. And He's always listening. Getting in the habit of continually praying teaches us, grows us, and rewards us with the joy of living freely and lightly. And divine joy is our strength.

Strength to face fears. Strength to encourage others. Strength to manage emotions. Strength to be brave, forgive, and love. *Strength to be more like Him*. So, here's to having a day filled with intimate moments and honest conversations with our Father and Friend and learning how to live freely and lightly in God's perfect, steadfast care.

FATHER, KEEPING COMPANY WITH YOU
KEEPS ME JOYFUL AND STRONG.
THANK YOU FOR ALWAYS BEING THERE.

LIGHTHOUSE OF LIFE

*When you go through
deep waters and great trouble,
I will be with you.*

ISAIAH 43:2 TLB

God is with us *when* we go through deep waters and great trouble, not *if* we do. Whether it be a pandemic, natural disaster, or civil unrest, it's important to know we're not alone and to understand that we have a beautiful opportunity to be there for the people God brings into our lives—those who might not know He's always with us and those who might be losing sight of it. There's a reason for paths crossing, lives intersecting, and brief encounters. Our strength, joy, and confidence can become life preservers in a world shaken by great troubles. A word spoken, a smile given, or a joyful spirit can be banners saying, *"It's going to be okay. God is with us."*

Rip currents are familiar to those of us who live near the ocean and are frequent beachgoers. Daily advisories report the level of risk for these currents. When the risk is high, they

warn not to swim because getting caught in a rip current can lead to being carried out into deep waters quickly with little or no control. For inexperienced or lone swimmers, it can be terrifying and even life threatening. In the same way, it can be frightening to feel alone in life's troubles pulled to a place of feeling overwhelmed and helpless.

But knowing Jesus, we know this: "God is our refuge and strength, an ever-present help in trouble" (PSALM 46:1 NIV). We are lighthouses now. Our actions can lead others to safe refuge. Our words can be lifesavers. Our prayers can change the course of lives being pulled away from the only hope we have. Today might bring people and circumstances we didn't expect—but this gives you have the opportunity to be courageous, bring joy, shine truth, and show love.

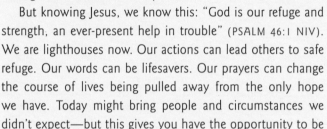

FATHER, YOU GUIDE EVERY STEP I TAKE TODAY.
I GIVE ALL OF ME TO SHINE A LIGHT ON ALL
OF YOU SO THAT EVERYONE AROUND ME SEES
HOPE, JOY, KINDNESS, AND LOVE.

SEARCHED AND SEEN

Search me, O God,
and know my heart; Try me,
and know my anxieties.

PSALM 139:23 NKJV

At the ocean is one of the few places on earth where our soul seems to whisper: *"Just breathe. God is bigger than every worry. God is greater than any fear. God is closer than the breath I'm taking."* He knows us. He knows our deepest struggles and understands our weaknesses. He knows what causes our anxious thoughts and how tempting it is for us to dwell on them to the point of consuming our minds and crowding out the truth. When we ask Him to search our hearts, we invite Him to change us in the best possible ways. We throw open the doors to every part of us to let His light expose things we've swept into corners, maybe because we haven't been ready, or willing, to face them.

When God searches us and reveals areas of our lives that need His strength and our surrender, it leads to spiritual growth spurts. And every bit of that growth gets us closer to who we truly are, the purpose we're truly made for, and the reflection of Jesus we truly want to be. When God is showing us how to build our spiritual muscles, it's a process that teaches us the discipline of complete trust and perfect rest.

The rewards we enjoy are fewer sleepless nights, less stressful days, and a lot more hope to carry us through even when the going does get tough. Trust is the spiritual muscle that needs a daily workout if we want to get the rest our minds and bodies yearn for. If we want the kind of relaxation that refreshes us on every level, we have to believe that whatever the day brings God has already *seen*—and He's given us a promise to quiet the anxious thoughts and a truth to strengthen every part of our hearts.

FATHER, YOU SEE ME AS I AM AND
LOVE ME MORE THAN I UNDERSTAND—
I TRUST YOU TO SHOW ME HOW TO GROW
BEYOND MY ANXIOUS THOUGHTS
AND INTO YOUR PERFECT REST.
TEACH ME TO TRUST YOU MORE THAN
I EVER HAVE BEFORE.

KNOWING JOY

The whole earth is filled
with awe at Your wonders;
where morning dawns,
where evening fades,
You call forth songs of joy.

PSALM 65:8 NIV

I love music. When I go to the beach there's always a wireless speaker in my bag. I've watched the sunrise on Easter morning while belting out "My Redeemer Lives" and crying like a baby through the whole song. *I love beach people.* They're laid back and too absorbed in God's stunning, miraculous, and magnificent creation to judge me or my vocal prowess. *I love divine joy.* It's not a feeling and it's not what the world calls happiness. It's being convinced of God's goodness and determined to trust His faithfulness even when it looks like everything that can go wrong *is* going wrong. It's the deep-down *knowing* part of us that brings deep-down joy.

God, I *know* You love me. God, I *know* You'll take care of me. God, I *know* You're bigger than this problem. God, I *know* You won't leave me. God, I *know* You're my hope. God, I *know* You're the only hope I need! We can get through life without a lot of things, but we can't get through it without hope—and joy is a beautiful by-product of it. I don't think it's possible to watch the sun come up in the morning and not be filled with hope. I'm always instantly thankful for the grace that comes with it, for God giving us another fresh start and for a brand new batch of hope to carry us through.

No matter what today looks like or what tomorrow would like us to worry about, we can choose an attitude of awe at our wonder-creating Father. We can be joyful about who He is and what we know He'll do. And maybe we'll turn on some music to go with all of our joy, and then sing out loud without a care in the world.

FATHER, I'LL LOOK FOR YOUR WONDERS
ALL AROUND ME TODAY, IN FACES, NATURE,
SKY, AND ALL THE LITTLE THINGS TOO—
AND MY HEART WILL BE THANKFUL FOR
THE JOY THAT COMES WITH THEM.

LIFE WITH GOD

IS NOT IMMUNITY

FROM DIFFICULTIES,

BUT PEACE

IN DIFFICULTIES.

—C.S. LEWIS

OUR PPS FOR PERFECT REST

Come to Me.
Get away with Me and
you'll recover your life.
I'll show you how to
take a real rest.

MATTHEW 11:28 THE MESSAGE

Being in a beach state of mind is relaxing. Being in a Jesus state of mind is *real rest*. The only way to recover the life we've been designed to live is by keeping our focus on the One who created us and taking our eyes off of worldly expectations. Sometimes even the people closest to us unintentionally make us feel we should be doing more or serving God in a different way.

Jesus likes to teach us one-on-one. We can listen to the counsel of loved ones and consider the wisdom of trusted friends, but the best way for us to follow God's perfectly fitting plan for our lives is by staying close to Him. His Word is His greatest teaching tool. It's full of life and it'll lead us to our *best* life! The more we allow His truth to become part of us, the lighter the weight of this world gets. The purpose we're here to fulfill becomes the life we live every day and with that comes peace and contentment. It feels right because it *is* right—it's exactly what Jesus had in mind for us to do.

Have you ever been driving and tried to listen to a passenger talk while concentrating on what the GPS is telling you to do? It's impossible to follow directions while listening to someone else's voice. Think of Jesus as our PPS, or Personal Positioning System. His direction is the only one we need to follow. Unlike the Global Positioning System that sometimes fails to get us where we need to be, our PPS will *never* fail to get us where we need to be in our lives.

Jesus is always with us. The plan He has for our lives is always good and guided by love. If we get away with Him, listen closely, and let Him lead, we won't get lost and our lives will stay on course in the center of His will—which is exactly where we want to be.

FATHER, THANK YOU FOR LEADING ME
THROUGH MY DAY WITH YOUR LOVE AND TRUTH.
IF I GET DISCOURAGED OR DISTRACTED REMIND ME
THAT REAL REST COMES BY TRUSTING YOU.

THE BELONGING
BETWEEN

The earth is the Lord's,
and everything in it, the world,
and all who live in it.

PSALM 24:1 NIV

A sense of belonging is a natural desire for all of us. We feel it because we were created with a need to know and love God. Even though there isn't a living thing on this earth that doesn't *belong* to God, our deepest sense of *belonging* can only be satisfied by accepting the gift of eternal life through the person of Jesus. He's love, peace, hope, and light. He's comfort, strength, courage, and joy. He's Friend, Savior, Father, and King. He's all we need, and every part of creation reveals Him to us.

How is it that we still have days when we feel like we don't belong? We wake up and follow routines robotically. We try to refuel hopes we hold deep inside by believing this could be the day something changes. Today God will reveal

the surprising news. Today we'll get the email or the phone call we've been waiting for. Today the answers we've prayed for will be as clear as tropical ocean waters and the next steps we take as sure as the waves hitting the shore.

Then the day plays out nearly as identical as the one before, and we fall into bed feeling more alone than we ever have. We feel less like we belong to any plan or any *one*, including the One who holds the earth and everything in it. We're fickle and forgetfully human, until the Holy Spirit and our aching hearts remind us that we not only *belong* to God, we are His *beloved*.

> *Let the beloved of the Lord rest secure in Him, for He shields him all day long, and the one the Lord loves rests between His shoulders.* DEUTERONOMY 33:12 NIV

Is there a place in the entire universe we could feel a greater sense of belonging than when we *rest between the shoulders of God; secure, shielded, and loved*? What a breathtaking visual of our eternal belonging, and what a beautiful reminder to carry us through the day.

FATHER, I LOVE THE TRUTH THAT I BELONG TO YOU
AND THAT YOUR PURPOSE FOR MY LIFE
FULFILLS EVERY SENSE OF BELONGING I HAVE.
I KNOW YOU WORK EVERYTHING TOGETHER
FOR GOOD IN YOUR PERFECT WAY AND TIME.

THE GIFT IN THE WAIT

Rest in the Lord;
wait patiently for Him to act.

PSALM 37:7 TLB

Resting while we're waiting doesn't sound like the best use of our time. There must be something we can do to hurry things along, right? This isn't waiting in line at a drive-through, waiting to be seen at the dentist's office, or waiting for the oven to preheat. This is waiting while God works all things together for good. This is waiting to see the promises of God come to fruition in our lives. This is waiting for God to act while staying confident, courageous, and humble. God is working in our lives every single day, but there are *lots* of days that require us to wait quietly and thankfully until His plan comes together. In fact, those days are collectively referred to as "seasons" by wise souls who've spent a lifetime serving God.

The resting He asks us to do is trusting that He *will* do—what is most loving, what is most glorifying, and what matures us most *spiritually*. Knowing God more leads to growing us more. The abundant life He has for us isn't about possessions or position. It isn't measured by social media influence, number of likes, or how much traffic a website gets in a day. The real abundance in life comes when we discover *He is all we need*. We rise in the wait, not the arrival.

Dreams—God-orchestrated dreams—are coming. They're going to be more than we hoped for. But through the long days of waking up with a still-aching heart, when nothing is happening in the natural and it feels like God has turned His back on us, in truth, He's drawing us closer to His side. We're learning to lean on the promises of heaven no matter what we see or how long it takes. We're learning to draw from God's strength and stand in His presence. During the wait we reach the highest place we'll ever be by seeing that our heart's desire is never the dream we have, but *Him*.

FATHER, I WON'T GIVE UP ON THE PROMISES
YOU'VE GIVEN. REVEAL TO ME THE THINGS
I NEED TO LEARN AND THE WAYS I NEED TO GROW
WHILE I WAIT FOR THE GOOD THINGS COMING.
I BELIEVE THEY'LL BE MORE THAN I IMAGINED.

THREE LITTLE WORDS

*His peace will keep your thoughts
and your hearts quiet and at rest
as you trust in Christ Jesus.*

PHILIPPIANS 4:7 TLB

*A*s *we trust*. Three little words to keep in the forefront of our minds today. Three little words to keep our thoughts calm and quiet. Three little words to give our hearts a rest from whatever is causing the pain, sadness, or fear. *As we trust* in Christ Jesus, peace comes to soothe our hurts and silence our worries. The first part of this verse from Philippians encourages us: "Don't worry about anything; instead, pray about everything."

Long walks along the beach are great times to reflect and pray about everything. The vastness of the ocean carries our thoughts to a place of thankfulness and hope, to a renewed appreciation for our Father, and to the absolute joy of knowing Him. How does anyone get through life and the trials of this world without running straight to the shelter of His love? God's love is the only thing that has the strength and resilience to

rescue us *every* time. Picture yourself walking on the shoreline and watching the waves—don't they just emulate the flow of life? At one point they roll onto shore in a calm, soothing way, and before long they crash in with a thunderous roar. They can be unpredictable and startling as life often is. But we have to keep walking, be it calm or chaotic, and trust God will guide us through it all.

More than ever before we need the peace He gives to keep our hearts at rest whether life comes softly or with a harshness we weren't expecting. As we trust, our worries subside. As we pray, God covers everything. As we hold onto Him, hope holds on inside of us. A tough day can be followed by a great one because God is busy loving everything into place in every area of our lives. He's good all the time and gracious with our weaknesses. Our circumstances don't get the last say, God does. And He's *trustworthy*—no matter how the waves come in today.

FATHER, I TRUST YOU
WITH EVERYTHING IN MY LIFE.
WHEN MY HEART BEGINS TO FEEL OVERWHELMED,
I THANK YOU FOR REMINDING ME
THAT WORRIES ARE NOT FOR ME TO CARRY
AND YOU ARE MY PEACE.

GRATEFUL HEART, GRITTY FAITH

*How refreshed I am
by Your blessings!*

PSALM 92:10 TLB

Have you ever started a gratitude journal? It's a way to put yourself in the good habit of writing down five things you're grateful for every day. And it's one of the best ways to be mindful of how many beautiful things God puts in our lives—things we forget to give attention to or routinely take for granted. His goodness is all around us all the time, but we still fall human and lose sight of His constant and caring presence. With a gratitude journal we can go through and see God's nearness and faithfulness time and time again. We can smile big, stay thankful, and get a boost of confidence to walk out the door and overcome any fear or doubt in front of us.

Our worries are short-lived if we rewind God's victories in our lives. The one when He moved everything into place at the right time for the job we needed, or the time when a friend called with every word we needed to hear when we needed to hear it, or the time when we were holding onto our last thread of hope and God provided more than enough. God shows up when we refuse to give up. He honors a grateful heart and a gritty faith. "For the eyes of the Lord run to and fro throughout the whole earth, to show Himself strong on behalf of those whose heart is loyal to Him" (2 CHRONICLES 16:9 NKJV). *God will not fail us!*

Every blessing He's given us is a source of spiritual refreshment and strength for our soul. They're the tangible, touchable things that grow our faith and build our courage for what's ahead. His blessings will keep coming, as will our trials. But knowing we'll meet the trials with a strong heart that is loyal to God means we have *nothing* to fear. He's watching closely to show Himself strong on our behalf! *That's* a refreshing blessing.

FATHER, MY FAITH IS STRENGTHENED
BY EVERY BLESSING YOU GIVE
AND EVERY PROMISE YOU KEEP.
THANK YOU FOR BEING MY STRONG FORTRESS
AND LOVING ME COMPLETELY.

SHIFTING OUR LOAD

Yes, my soul, find rest in God;
my hope comes from Him.

PSALM 62:5 NIV

Rest can feel like an impossible thing to accomplish on a regular basis in our everyday lives. There's always so much to keep us on the run. There are too many lists to look at, to-dos to get done, and demands to attend to. Our bodies need rest to be restored and energized, but our spirits need rest to keep our bodies *well*. That's why God encourages us to rest and give Him every care, even the ones we've gotten in the habit of picking up again and again. Not only does the "picking up" weigh us down, it holds us back from the beautiful freedom Jesus provided. He sacrificed everything so that through grace all the heavy lifting is done for us. When we take His way and His will, we don't get worn out.

We can leave fear at His feet with the confidence: "God has not given us a spirit of fear, but of power and love and of a sound mind" (2 TIMOTHY 1:7 NKJV). We can leave lack in the grip of His promise: "You can be sure that God will take care of everything you need, His generosity exceeding

even yours in the glory that pours from Jesus" (PHILIPPIANS 4:19 THE MESSAGE). We can leave self-doubt and insecurity beneath the certainty: "With God, everything is possible" (MATTHEW 19:26 TLB).

There will always be enough. He will always be our courage. We are going to see the desires He placed in our hearts *come to pass*. Giving our spirit the rest it needs will give our mind the break it needs to face the day with the hope the world needs to see. If we let God lighten our mental load today, we'll have room for His love to flow through us even more.

FATHER, I GIVE YOU MY CARES AND ALL
THE MENTAL CLUTTER THAT KEEPS ME FROM
LOVING AND SERVING YOU COMPLETELY—
SPIRIT, SOUL, AND BODY. HELP ME SEE
THE NEEDS AROUND ME BY TRUSTING
ALL OF MINE TO YOU.

WAY TO SHINE!

*The path of the just
is like the shining sun.*

PROVERBS 4:18 NKJV

God is love and love is *bright*. Kindness and love leave trails of light in our lives that become brighter as we draw closer to their source. Our presence, or rather His presence in us, starts to feel like pure sunshine to everyone we come in contact with. And who doesn't want to be sunshine in a dark world? On sunny days it seems like joy explodes. Birds sing a little more exuberantly, smiles increase, moods lift, and optimism comes a little easier. Light has a positive effect on our overall well-being. I think it's another reason why blue-sky, beach days are so healing. It's impossible to be unhappy there!

Our heartfelt desire should be that the path of our lives stay flooded by the light of God. Love, joy, peace, patience, kindness, goodness, faithfulness, gentleness and self-control are the things that keep it illuminated. We won't get everything right every day, but we *will* get new mercy every morning. If one day dims our path, the next can make it shine again because we walk in grace and forgiveness. God will never hold His hand over the light of our lives when we fail. His love will lift us right back up and into the spotlight that points to Him. We're created in His image and that's a humbling thought. But it's also a refreshing reminder that His glory can light the world through us.

The way to shine is by letting God have His way with our days, our actions, our choices, and our hearts. A little prayer of surrender before we move through our day goes a long way in keeping the path of our lives well-lit by loving well. The best days are always about how we love the people in our lives in the best ways. Nothing else lights up lives like the love of God, and nothing on earth is more fulfilling than being the one it shines through.

FATHER, SHINE BRIGHTLY
THROUGH MY LIFE TODAY,
DRAWING EYES AND HEARTS TO YOU
BY THE WARMTH OF YOUR LOVE.

CHILDLIKE TRUST

How kind He is! How good He is!
So merciful, this God of ours!
The Lord protects the simple
and the childlike.

PSALM 116:5-6 TLB

My God, let my life be a proof of what the omnipotent God can do. Let these be the two dispositions of our souls every day—deep helplessness and simple, childlike rest.

—ANDREW MURRAY

Can we remember? Building a sandcastle without a care in the world about how long it takes or how many times we have to start over. Picking up shells until our fists are full without thinking about carrying anything else, including a single worry. Running into the waves without fear of being knocked down and having a fierce determination to get back up if we do. Childlike ways. They're worth nurturing. God loves the simplicity of a child's heart, which is why He encourages us

to rekindle ours. Even as grown-ups we're still His children, whether or not we choose to remain simple and childlike.

I recall a time when I was on an extremely turbulent flight on a small plane. The pilot had decided to land in severe weather. Clearly, the adults onboard were not in agreement that this would end well. There were faces, and hearts, wrenched with fear. I'll admit I was having a hard time handling *my* fear, until I noticed a young boy across the aisle and a couple rows ahead of me. He was sound asleep. I could see his head bouncing up and down with every bump and sway, but he stayed peacefully unaware and unaffected. *Wow*, I thought. That's what trusting the pilot looks like. How much more should I trust the pilot of my soul, the One who's in control of *all* my days?

God showed me that day what childlike trust looks like. I could hear Him whisper, *"That's how sure of Me I want you to be."* He understands how hard life is and how tempting it is for us to be anything but simple and childlike. Our responsibilities are on replay in the middle of the night and negative news reels come at us in the middle of the day. Adult things can suffocate our childlike spirit. *That's why we have to remember:* Our Father protects us, our Father loves us, and *no one will snatch us out of His hand.*

FATHER, GIVE ME THE FEARLESSNESS OF CHILDLIKE TRUST.

Setting apart a day
of rest testifies
to a self-reliant world
that our work does
not save or define us.

God does.

—JOHN PIPER

TURNING OUR THOUGHTS

He will keep in perfect peace all those who trust in Him, whose thoughts turn often to the Lord!

ISAIAH 26:3 TLB

Beach sounds woo our hearts and minds into a quiet, restful state. The waves and the breeze are constant, like the peace of God constantly inviting us to rest in Him. Every day won't go as planned. Our lives won't be free from pain. Our journey will not look exactly the way we dreamed it would. But God's peace will keep us. It will be constant on the days when unexpected news comes and fills our heart with fear. It will be constant when we lose someone we deeply love. God's peace will keep us and guide us through the steps of our lives even though we don't see things unfold when or how we imagined.

We can have a steady, constant peace when life goes up, down, or sideways because God is the master of our days.

He's also the One who knows us best and loves us most. There's no one in our life more trustworthy. Even on the disappointing, difficult days when it's nearly impossible to believe, He's in the center of our being doing what it takes to make the painting of our lives *more* beautiful than we imagined. That's what God's love does. It brings out the breathtakingly beautiful parts in all of us and produces a fulfilling, faithful life that reflects His glory.

We have a lot to think about from day to day, but if our everyday lives don't have us turning our thoughts *often* to our only hope, we won't be able to enjoy His perfect peace. God is in constant listening mode when it comes to His children. He's never too busy or distracted or tired. He can keep us steady and peaceful if our thoughts become prayers. "Show me how to handle this, it's not going to be easy. Help me stay calm and be kind. Lord, give me wisdom for the conversation I need to have and give me the courage to speak what needs to be said." Our need for our Father is all day long, in all things. There's perfect peace in turning *often* to Him—and it's always worth it.

FATHER, GIVE ME THE COURAGE TO KEEP
MY TRUST IN YOU AS I KEEP TURNING
TO YOU THROUGHOUT MY DAY.

LETTING GO OF THE REINS

I love the Lord because He hears my prayers and answers them. Because He bends down and listens, I will pray as long as I breathe!

PSALM 116:1-2 TLB

It's comforting to be heard. When we have a conversation and know a friend is truly listening, it feels like a respite for our heart. It feels like a sigh of relief for our soul. It feels like some of the weight we've been carrying is lifted. We all go through lonely times when we're sure no one can possibly know or understand our personal struggles. But God is bending down to listen closely and let us know He's always close. He wants us to talk to Him and be open about the things He knows we're going through, because knowing He hears is strengthening *us*.

Praying puts us in God's presence, and no matter the size of our need or the battle we face, the courage to win is coming when we spend time with Him. We win in life by going to the creator of life and trusting He's leading the charge through every trial, because He *is*. And the timing of the battle's end is also His—the challenge to *rest* in His perfect timing is ours.

Learning to relax and let God take the reins of our life and everything in it is never going to be easy. Our flesh likes to grab hold and share the control. It's very human of us to look at our circumstances and think we can "go this one alone," but it's never a good idea. *Pray about everything.* That's wisdom. And wisdom is *always* a good idea. In truth, it's the best idea because it gets God involved. We don't want to simply believe He sees everything and knows everything; we want to ask Him to be a part of *every* aspect of our lives in order to guide, teach, and shape us. Our transformation for God's glorification. Our lives will light up this world if we humbly let Him lead.

FATHER, I LOVE THAT YOU HEAR ME,
AND I TRUST THAT YOU'LL LEAD ME IN THE WAY
THAT'S BEST FOR MY GROWTH AND YOUR GLORY.

STRENGTHENED, REFRESHED, AND REVIVED!

Never forget Your promises to me...for they are my only hope. They give me strength in all my troubles; how they refresh and revive me!

PSALM 119:49-50 TLB

There are a lot of worldly solutions coming at us every day when we hope to lose weight, be successful, live longer, look younger, and the list goes on and on. I'm so thankful God is our only source of hope for all the things we truly need and all the goals that matter most. Love others. Show kindness. Be compassionate. Be patient. Stay joyful. Give selflessly. Be thankful. Be a light. Trust fully. Be courageous and don't give up. God's list of reasons to be hopeful and ways we should hope to become goes on and on too, but it's a list of things that will have an eternal impact, not a temporal one.

Our bodies are temples and should be respected and cared for, but the things that affect us spiritually are far more important. When we learn to depend on God to keep His promises and give us strength in all our troubles, we become a spiritual force to be reckoned with. Earthly goals are shadowed by eternal gains. Both are valuable. One is *priceless*.

When we lean into the promises of God our lives are filled "with good things so that our youth is renewed like the eagle's" (PSALM 103:5 NIV). We're refreshed and revived! We're the light leading the world to the One who gives all the hope any of us will ever need. And God will start bringing people into our lives that need real hope, because we've strengthened our spirit by trusting Him. We've grown confident in being still and knowing He's God. We've become less shaken by what's going on around us and more certain of Who's in us. We exude hope and joy, and we've gotten better at loving others the way He loves us, with mercy, with compassion, and without condition.

FATHER, YOU ARE MY HOPE. YOUR FAITHFULNESS HAS GIVEN ME STRENGTH I DIDN'T KNOW I HAD. GIVE ME MORE OF YOU SO THERE'S LESS OF ME IN EVERY AREA OF MY LIFE.

CHARTED IN DETAIL

You chart the path ahead of me
and tell me where to stop
and rest. Every moment
You know where I am.

PSALM 139:3 TLB

The beach I go to regularly is close to home and uncrowded. I love it. There are rock formations along the shoreline and when the waves crash into them gorgeous blue foam formations shoot straight into the air. Once, I caught a photo of one that was shaped like a heart. Glimpses of God's love are everywhere when we look for them, and nowhere are they more moving and powerful than in the things He created.

I have a turnaround point on my beach walks. It's a little museum called The House of Refuge. It, too, reminds me of our Father. He's our safe refuge in any storm, through any circumstance, and at any time. I didn't realize until recently that this beach changes drastically with the erosion that occurs during hurricane season. On one of my visits, I couldn't walk where I usually do because the sand had been pulled

away by the rough surf, revealing a series of rocks I'd never seen before. I didn't know that all this time I'd been walking over this impassable place safely, only because it was buried in sand.

It made me think of the way God charts the path of our lives. We can't always see the underlying dangers of taking steps or making choices, but He can. That's why our best life depends on asking Him to chart our path and tell us where to stop and rest, or when to move forward.

God sees every moment of our journey. He knows every part of who we are. He knows the way we should go to intersect with every life He planned for us to touch. After all, that's all that matters, the way our relationship with Him affects our relationships *here*. God *charts* our path, which means He *watches with careful attention or records in detail*. Every day of our life has meaning, a message, and a map—it's up to us to consult the One who knows every detail perfectly.

FATHER, LEAD ME TO THE PLACES, THE NEEDS,
AND THE LIVES YOU PLANNED FOR ME TO SERVE.
I ASK YOU TO MAKE MY PATH SAFE
AND MY HEART PREPARED.

STRENGTH IN A TIRED PLACE

I'll refresh tired bodies;
I'll restore tired souls.

JEREMIAH 31:25 THE MESSAGE

It's okay to have tired days, when you don't get a lot accomplished or feel like you have the energy you need. Our souls get weary and our bodies get tired. God understands. "He is like a Father to us, tender and sympathetic to those who reverence Him. For He knows we are but dust" (PSALM 103:13-14 TLB). The way to reset our spirit, soul, and body to a beach-rested, restored, and refreshed state is by depending on God's life in us. It's infallible, vibrant, loving, and strong. It's complete healing, perfect peace, exuberant joy and eternal hope. It's the good stuff that brings back the determination we need to keep running the race. "Let us run with patience the particular race that God has set before us" (HEBREWS 12:1 TLB).

There's grace for our tired days and there's goodness in taking time to simply rest in it. God's grace is sufficient to carry us through the down times and the discouragement we all face. Life isn't easy. Trials come and we dig deep for the strength to get through them, and we find it's always in the same place. God brings strength and hope to our rescue every time. There isn't anything He *can't* or *won't* do for us, no matter how worn out we are from the pace of this life and the challenges it holds.

When we've done all we can to stand, God will give us everything we need to keep our knees from buckling. We're going to get through because God is going to redeem everything. And He's going to replenish us—our tired souls, our aching hearts, and our downcast spirits. He's our unfailing Father. He's our unrelenting hope. He will do what He's promised, and He will never, ever forsake us. Amen to being absolutely sure our brightest days are coming, friend.

FATHER, BE THE COMFORT AND
STRENGTH IN OUR WEARINESS TODAY.
YOUR PRESENCE EMPOWERS US AND
GIVES US THE COURAGE TO TRUST
AND KEEP GOING.

GRAINS OF SAND, OCEAN WATERS, AND SKIES OF BLUE

How precious to me are Your thoughts, God! How vast is the sum of them! Were I to count them, they would outnumber the grains of sand.

PSALM 139:17-18 NIV

What, or who, is consuming your thought life today? The answer will determine what kind of day is ahead. If there's a problem that looks insurmountable, a struggle to forgive someone, a feeling of loneliness, an endless list of things to do, the *first* thing to do is to keep putting Jesus first! If we put every thought in line behind Him and remind ourselves that He thinks about us constantly, our soul's sigh of relief comes. We're on His mind and there isn't a single thing we can do to stop the avalanche of love coming into our lives *right now*.

74

God's love is the only thing we should allow to overwhelm us. It's unstoppable and all-encompassing. It's constant and comforting. It's in *every* thought He has of us, and those thoughts outnumber the grains of sand. And what does love do? Love does what is best, love does whatever is patient and kind, love does everything it can and more than enough. YOU are what Jesus is thinking about! He sees any turmoil going on in your heart, mind, and life, and He has loving truth to cover it all:

> *I am leaving you with a gift—peace of mind and heart. And the peace I give is a gift the world cannot give. So don't be troubled or afraid.* JOHN 14:27 NLT

> *Peace will guard your hearts and minds as you live in Christ Jesus.* PHILIPPIANS 4:7 NLT

> *God has not given us a spirit of fear, but of power and of love and of a sound mind.* 2 TIMOTHY 1:7 NKJV

We can't let fear have the last say today because we're loved higher, wider, and deeper than it can ever go. The grains of sand, the ocean waters and the skies of blue can't come close to measuring God's love for us. When our thoughts begin with Him, our days begin to get better. The only thing mandatory is letting Jesus manage everything, allowing His love to keep our hearts and minds at peace.

FATHER, LET YOUR LOVE COME AND
OVERTAKE ME TODAY, SO THAT ALL OF
MY THOUGHTS TURN TO YOU.

IN STEP WITH SUFFICIENT GRACE

Learn the unforced rhythms of grace.

MATTHEW 11:29 THE MESSAGE

Picture yourself on the beach, watching the sun pop up and its big yellow face breaking the horizon to light the ocean and sky at once. Doesn't this mental picture just move your heart? Now, listen closely and you'll hear God say, "Here you go. A brand-new day with all the grace you'll need to live it." He doesn't bring up mistakes. He doesn't point out weaknesses. He doesn't do anything but throw open His merciful, east-to-west reaching arms and love us. And there's nothing forced about the love or grace He gives. He truly, wholeheartedly, eternally loves us; and He freely, generously, genuinely provides grace through the sacrifice of His Son. We have favor and blessing that we did not and could not earn.

All of our days bring challenges. No matter what they turn out to be, we walk in step with enough grace to handle and overcome them. We don't need to strive or reach into tomorrow's grace to borrow a little. We don't have grace for worrying about what's coming next week. God gives sufficient grace to conquer our days as fast as we can live them—one at a time. As soon as we get there, we'll walk in the beautiful rhythm of God's daily plans for us, which is in perfect step with His love for us.

Staying in our moments and days without jumping ahead mentally isn't easy. It doesn't come naturally. We learn to be present. We learn to surrender to God. We learn to go with the flow of grace instead of fighting against it with fear, worry, or self-reliance. God is the strength of our heart, and we are the chosen, blessed, and thankful recipients of His *amazing* grace. So, when the sun sets on another day, I hope we watch it go knowing we'll never exhaust the mercy and grace that's coming to greet us with the dawn.

FATHER, THANK YOU FOR GIVING
EVERY OUNCE OF GRACE NEEDED
TO LIVE TODAY TRUSTING YOU FULLY,
SERVING YOU JOYFULLY, AND LOVING YOU
WITH ALL OF MY HEART, SOUL, AND MIND.

OUR WELL OF REFRESHMENT

*I restore the crushed
in spirit of the humble
and revive the courage of those
with repentant hearts.*

ISAIAH 57:15 NLT

A good way to discover how humble we *aren't* is by deciding to love someone we don't like very much. Even if it's "not very much" in the moment. We can use all kinds of reasons and excuses: I think so differently than they do; I can't handle being around someone who talks so loudly; I'm offended by x, y, and z. The underlying problem and common denominator in all of those reasons is "I." And the first rule of loving people the way God loves people is that it's never about me, myself, *or* I.

> *Love suffers long and is kind; love does not envy;
> love does not parade itself, is not puffed up; does not
> behave rudely, does not seek its own, is not provoked,
> thinks no evil; does not rejoice in iniquity, but rejoices*

in the truth; bears all things, believes all things, hopes
all things, endures all things. Love never fails.
1 CORINTHIANS 13:4-8 NKJV

It doesn't sound like humility hangs out in the things love *does not* do, parade, puff up, seek its own, rejoice in iniquity. Choosing to love often takes a whole lot of courage and humility. More than we can muster on our own. Thankfully, God promises to refresh those qualities in us when we come to Him with repentant hearts. The way to get the "I" out of love's way is to go to the One who *is* love and ask for forgiveness. We are all guilty of asking, "Everybody? There are no exceptions? But, but...."

The answer is there *are* no exceptions, and there's also no room for ifs, ands, buts, or whys when it comes to loving every person in our lives. It's something we do because we have love's perfect, powerful, and perpetual source in us. God loves us always and unconditionally, no matter how unlovable *we* are at times, and that's our gracious starting point. "As I have loved you, so you must love one another" (JOHN 13:34 NIV). Let's go to God, our well of refreshment, and love everybody in our lives with courage and humility today.

FATHER, I ASK YOU TO REFRESH MY HEART
WITH THE QUALITIES OF YOUR LOVE AND
SHOW ME IF THERE'S PRIDE IN ME THAT
NEEDS TO BE REPLACED WITH HUMILITY.
GIVE ME COURAGE TO LOVE LIKE YOU DO.

Isn't it comfort to worship a God we cannot exaggerate?

—FRANCIS CHAN

REST IN THE STORM

He stilled the storm
to a whisper; the waves
of the sea were hushed.

PSALM 107:29 NIV

Trials aren't easy. Tests aren't fun. But our spiritual growth is more valuable than we'll fully understand in this life. We're learning to love God more and love others better. And even when it feels like too much, Jesus knows exactly when to still the storm and hush the waves. He's never late to our rescue. We're *growing* and we're *going* to get through.

Our part in the process is to *relax*, rest in God, and take courage from our perfect example, who fell asleep in the back of the boat while the storm raged. We don't have to see or know how the storm will end, we just have to trust with all our heart and soul that it will. And on the other side of it our faith will be stronger, our hearts will be braver, and our lives will be brighter.

Have you ever taken a walk on the beach when the sand is hard? What about when it's soft? One is much easier than the other, but the one that's more difficult builds more muscle and burns more calories. In the end, the tougher path is far better. The same goes for our life path. The more challenging the trials the stronger we become, and with God in the lead there's going to be a beautiful outcome. The best result. Each one will get us closer to a clearer reflection of Him. For us that means less fear and more faith, less doubt and more confidence, less discouragement and more hope. And hope that can't be extinguished, even in the worst of storms, can change the world.

FATHER, I KNOW THE STORMS
WILL COME AND GO IN MY LIFE,
AND I KNOW YOU'RE WITH ME
THROUGH THEM ALL.
REFRESH MY HOPE AND STRENGTHEN ME
TO FACE THEM WITH CONFIDENCE.
YOU KNOW WHEN TO STILL THEM
TO A WHISPER.

THE HOPE THAT KEEPS US HAPPY

God who gives you hope
will keep you happy and
full of peace as you
believe in Him.

ROMANS 15:13 TLB

Is it possible to be unhappy at the beach? There are children laughing, sandpipers scurrying, surfers surfing, dogs playing in the water, and an overall sense that everything is going to be okay. Most beachgoers are in a peaceful, relaxed mood—reading a book, taking a walk, meditating, or marveling at God's handiwork. The ocean's edge is a perfect spot for God-marveling. "Open your eyes and there it is! By taking a long and thoughtful look at what God has created, people have always been able to see what their eyes as such can't see: eternal power, for instance, and the mystery of His divine being" (ROMANS 1:20 THE MESSAGE).

God's awe-inspiring creation rekindles hope in us, and the hope God gives keeps us at peace. His hope makes its way into the deepest part of us when we *believe*. When we believe He is present and active in our lives. When we believe He is always loving us into the best place. When we believe He is our safe refuge in this not-so-easy, sometimes-scary world. We're happy when we're hopeful because in God's keep is where we *belong*. In His care is where we feel whole, protected, content, and refreshed. In Him, we feel like our most *authentic* self.

Every part of who we are needs every part of who God is. Every day we get to lean into that truth and trust. He gives us the hope we need to lift our spirit, build our courage, and boost our joy. God knows that hopeful, happy hearts make a lasting impression on the people we meet. And the hope He gives isn't based on a formula or a list of how-tos. It comes straight from the love that won't leave and can't fail. It comes from grace that says it's impossible for us to be separated from that love. It comes from the love that created us. And it's all *any* of us need to be contagiously happy.

FATHER, YOUR HOPE IS MY HAPPY!
FILL ME WITH PEACE AS I GIVE ALL MY CARE
AND WORRY TO YOU AND TRUST MY LIFE
WILL BE A LIGHT WHEREVER I GO.

A SOUL-REFRESHING REMINDER

A sweet friendship
refreshes the soul.

PROVERBS 27:9 THE MESSAGE

I've had many memorable and meaningful prayer times at the beach. When I was a caregiver for my parents, those few hours at the ocean every week pulled me through. It was the refreshment my soul needed. It was quality time with the greatest friend we have on earth, the One who knows us best and has every answer. Our heavenly Father not only listens without missing a word, He sees all the pain we can't put into words.

When we wake up every morning our worldly obligations come rushing in to fill our minds and get our bodies moving. Routines and responsibilities take over and before we know it, another day is gone. Then another week, month, and year pass and we wonder how we can slow down our lives just a little. We can't do that, of course, but we can be refreshed by knowing God recorded *all* of our days before we lived one of them—*so every single one of them matter.*

The home, the family, the friends, the meals, the laundry, the pets, the job, the shopping lists, the picking up toys, the wiping noses, the bedtime stories, the appointments, the helping neighbors, the errands, the one and a million things that make up our days matter, because every one of our lives mattered enough for Jesus to sacrifice His.

"Whatever you do, whether in word or deed, do it all in the name of the Lord Jesus, giving thanks to God" (COLOSSIANS 3:17 NIV). Nothing we do is small if we wrap it in His likeness and do it with compassion, kindness, humility, gentleness, and patience. And all of those virtues are bound together by love. When we start our days with the soul-refreshing reminder that love will never fail to make a difference in *everything* we do—and our best friend and heavenly Father wrote the script—we know that our moments have eternal significance no matter how fast they go. So, let's live every one of them with joy and gratefulness today.

FATHER, I'M REFRESHED BY YOUR FRIENDSHIP
AND THE JOY OF YOUR PRESENCE.
I WANT TO REMEMBER THAT EVERYTHING I DO
IS FOR YOU AND THE LOVE
IN MY ACTIONS HAS ETERNAL VALUE.

RUNNING TO
OUR HIDING PLACE

*God is a safe place to hide,
ready to help when we need Him.*

PSALM 46:1 THE MESSAGE

Did you have a "safe" place to hide as a child, where it was quiet, where you could be alone, and no one could find you? God is our grown-up hiding place. A quiet refuge where stresses and fear can't find us, and peace is never far away. We run to Him, lay all our struggles, questions, and doubts at His feet, and peace comes soon after with a big, spiritual hug. In Him we breathe a little easier, get the rest we need, and gain the strength to go on.

We'd be wise to cultivate the habit of running to our hiding place when we feel afraid, overwhelmed, or tired. We'll likely end up spending a lot of time there, and we'll end up strengthening a lot of our weaknesses. God knows us intimately, so I imagine running to Him looks different for each of us. Long walks on the beach or hiking trail. Driving with praise and worship turned up. The first cup of coffee in the morning before the house wakes up. It doesn't matter what our grown-up, earthly "hiding place" looks like, if it encourages us to dwell in the secret place of the Most High, it's an invaluable place to hang out.

What a gift it is to feel safe in this wild world. God wants us to be so sure of His presence that we make everyone around us sure of it too. He hopes our lives are so saturated with His love that love is the only thing that pours out of us—even when we're pressed for time, pushed to our limit, or pierced by the pain of suffering. Running to Him is the only way we keep from running on empty.

FATHER, BEING WITH YOU RESTORES
EVERY PART OF ME FOR WHAT
I'VE BEEN CREATED TO DO.
I WANT TO LEARN YOUR CHARACTER
BY SPENDING TIME AT YOUR SIDE.

HEMMED IN BY
BOUNDLESS LOVE

*You hem me in behind
and before, and You lay
Your hand upon me.*

PSALM 139:5 NIV

During the sea turtle season females come ashore to lay their clutch of around 100 eggs. The conservationist groups comb the beach every morning to look for signs of new nests. When they find one, they put brightly colored tape around it to alert beachgoers, so the newly discovered nests can remain safe and undisturbed. As a beachgoer, it's so nice to know these tiny sea turtle hatchlings are being protected. Our lives, in somewhat the same way, are hemmed in by God. Behind and before, His perfect love surrounds us, and His hand is always on our lives.

What a restful, comforting thought. We're enveloped by perfect love every moment, with God graciously protecting our peace, joy, and hope from being disturbed. The noise of the world will continue to go on all around us, but it has to cross the boundary of His truth to disrupt the peace we have in our Father's hand. There are plenty of temptations that can move us outside the circle of His perfect peace—worrying about things we can't change; fearing things we can't control; carrying the burdens we know we should give to Him.

Our desire should be to discipline our hearts and minds to stay inside the love that can conquer anything and change everything. When we fix our thoughts on His truth, we keep our focus on His love. His unfailing love hems us in on every side when we trust Him without wavering. And for the wobbling that inevitably happens? Grace. His hand is on us even when we fall, tenderly there to lift us up. "The Lord's unfailing love surrounds the one who trusts in Him" (PSALM 32:10 NIV). By living our lives wholly surrendered to God, the love surrounding us will let the world know it's the best and safest place to be.

FATHER, THANK YOU FOR
SURROUNDING ME WITH BOUNDLESS LOVE
AS I LEARN TO TRUST YOU FEARLESSLY EVERY DAY.

A SYMPHONY OF MIRACLES

You, Lord, are a shield around me.

PSALM 3:3 NIV

*You, Lord, will keep the needy safe
and will protect us forever.*

PSALM 12:7 NIV

Harmony is as refreshing as the dew.

PSALM 133:3 TLB

Sunrise on the beach is one of the most relaxing, rejuvenating, and inspiring things to experience. The pelicans start their morning flights over the water, the sun moves in perfectly timed increments, the ocean breeze pushes surface waves onto the shore, and it feels like every created thing around you is part of a breathtaking symphony. It's pure joy to watch miracles from God's hand in perfect harmony. It makes your heart swell with gratitude and overflow with praise. It makes you want to bottle the inspiration you feel and take it with you.

God desires our life in Him to move in harmony. He's promised to work everything together for our good and there's comfort in believing wholeheartedly that He will. But there are days. Days when it looks like the pieces of our life aren't in *any* kind of order. We grow tired of holding on and hoping. We grow weary of waiting for all the pieces and parts to fall into place. And sometimes, we're just plain tired.

These are the days God calls on us to sing from memory. To remember the last time we faced an impossible situation and He came in with perfect timing to write a beautiful lyric for our life. An inspirational, harmonious, miracle we could tuck into our hearts and recall over and over again. One He knew we would use to encourage a friend when they felt like giving up. God knows us, understands us, and loves us with all of His heart. Our tired souls don't surprise or disappoint Him. He's coming to our rescue. He's putting things in order. He's close. And every day we're a little closer to seeing the miracle He has in store.

FATHER, GIVE ME COURAGE TO KEEP GOING
AND GRATITUDE AS I LOOK BACK AT EVERYTHING
YOU'VE DONE FOR ME. REFRESH MY SPIRIT WITH
YOUR GOODNESS AND GIVE ME CONFIDENCE
IN YOUR PERFECT TIMING.

CHOSEN

You have been chosen
by God himself—you are priests
of the King, you are holy and
pure, you are God's very own—
all this so that you may show
to others how God called you
out of the darkness into
His wonderful light.

1 PETER 2:9 TLB

I sometimes forget to bring my shell bag to the beach and consequently end up filling my pockets with the unique, beautiful shells I can't resist picking up. I see them and find it impossible to leave them in the sand, their intricacies unappreciated. Isn't it amazing to know that God chose us? He sees us with an unlimited potential to make the world more beautiful. He brought us into His wonderful light to make our lives a shining example of His magnificent love. We belong to

Him, we're His beloved, and when He picked us up out of the mire and darkness, our names left an eternal *imprint* on the palm of His hand (ISAIAH 49:16).

When we go through tough seasons in life it can feel like we're the shells left in the sand. Unseen and walked past, our pain and heartache quietly ignored. In our hearts we know that's a terrible lie the enemy launches against everything we know is true of our Father. God is close to the brokenhearted and He feels our pain as deeply as we do. And He will *never* ignore the names inscribed on His hands. Our lives are a journey into His waiting arms, an incredible gift to be enjoyed and grateful for every step of the way. Even when the difficult parts get long and we get anxious, He's faithful to calm and comfort us.

The next time we feel unseen or it feels like our prayers aren't getting through, let's imagine God bending down to pick us up—because *He will*. He'll send a friend to encourage us. He'll put someone in our path to reveal His heart. Or He'll meet our need in the most unexpected way. "Even to your old age and gray hairs I am He, I am He who will sustain you. I have made you and I will carry you; I will sustain you and I will rescue you" (ISAIAH 46:4 NIV).

Remember that even in the challenges, we are the chosen and the carried.

FATHER, THANK YOU FOR PICKING ME UP
AND CARRYING ME THROUGH.

RUNNING IN THE RIGHT DIRECTION

True to Your word,
You let me catch my breath and
send me in the right direction.

PSALM 23:3 THE MESSAGE

Sandpipers are small birds that run along the shoreline foraging for food in the wet sand. They're also one of the cutest forms of entertainment on the beach. As soon as a wave recedes, they run toward the ocean to get all the yummy bits that wash in and then instinctively turn around and run away from the next wave before it touches their tiny feet. It's fascinating to watch their perfectly timed "dance" with the waves and the speed of their little legs! They never stay near the water too long, even though I'm sure it's tempting. They happily scurry away and wait patiently for the rhythm of the ocean to bring what they need, wave after wave after wave. They seem to understand an unfailing principle—their Creator will provide.

God will always guide us in the right direction for the things we need. We don't have to worry that He'll run out of options or get worn out by being faithful. Time and time again His trustworthy heart, filled with persevering love, brings the right-on-time provision without fail. And because we depend on Him and the truth of His word, we can relax, take a deep breath, and wait patiently for it. He won't let us down.

When discouragement tries to make a case against God's faithfulness, we have to go to His *true* word: "Your heavenly Father knows your needs. He will always give you all you need from day to day" (LUKE 12:30-31 TLB). When doubt tempts us, truth holds us: "God will meet all your needs according to the riches of His glory in Christ Jesus" (PHILIPPIANS 4:19 NIV). The world has changed tremendously since these words were recorded, but God has not changed, nor will He. When we run to Him, our provision is sure.

FATHER, YOU'RE TRUE TO YOUR WORD
AND I REST SAFELY IN IT TODAY.
HELP ME STAND STRONG, STAY HOPEFUL,
AND GO IN THE DIRECTION
YOU LEAD MY HEART TO GO.

YOU HEAVENS,

PRAISE HIM;

PRAISE HIM, EARTH;

ALSO OCEAN AND

ALL THINGS

THAT SWIM IN IT.

PSALM 69:34 THE MESSAGE

WISDOM IN 8 WORDS

*God wants His loved ones
to get their proper rest.*

PSALM 127:2 TLB

There's a popular Italian phrase from a famous movie—it's *dolce far niente*—the art of doing nothing. *Pleasant idleness.* In the context of the scene, a gentleman was passionately explaining that not everyone understands how to properly rest. My thought was, "He's *right!*" I think we like to stay on top of things and control as much of our life and time as we can. And I admit it's a challenge for me to let go and let God. But if we're going to debate how to rest properly, we can't leave God out of it. As a matter of fact, He has to be the center of it, or we aren't going to enjoy *any* real rest.

God wants us to rest. He created our bodies to need it. There are endless health benefits that come with releasing stress, disconnecting from work, and getting a good night's sleep. God wouldn't design us to need something that isn't found in Him. We're created in His image. We live and move and have our being in Him. But it's up to us to mentally and physically surrender to His perfect care. We've all been at the end of our day feeling exhausted and ready to fall into bed, and as soon as we do, the thought reel starts rolling. This reel is never cued by God so we can't let that happen if we want the sweet sleep that He promises.

A few years ago, I met an elderly gentleman who gave me his advice for getting good sleep. He told me he used the 8 after 8 routine every night. After 8 p.m., when it's time to start unwinding and think about going to bed, he prepared with 8 words: *give it to God and go to sleep*. He told me it had worked for him for as long as he could remember. I took it as good advice from a wise soul, and I've used it ever since.

FATHER, PROPER REST COMES BY TRUSTING YOU
WITH EVERYTHING THAT CONCERNS ME.
HELP ME CLEAR MY MIND AND ALLOW MY BODY
TO GET THE REST IT NEEDS.

OUR THOUGHTFUL INFLUENCE

Fix your thoughts on what is true and good and right.

PHILIPPIANS 4:8 TLB

Fix your thoughts on the ocean. Listen to the repetition of the waves. Fill your thoughts with blue sky. Feel the warmth of the sunshine on your face. Dig your toes into the soft sand. Our thoughts can transport us to the bliss of the beach in moments. Thoughts are powerful. Imagination is a gift. We get to choose what we focus them on. The demands of our day keep us focused on the task at hand, but what about the quiet hours? The times of reflection? That's when the steering becomes important. It takes a few minutes of watching the news to send our thoughts into a downward spiral, and if we're not careful, the images of everything that's going wrong in the world can take our mind hostage for too long.

Jesus said, "In this world you will have trouble. But take heart! I have overcome the world" (JOHN 16:33 NIV). When

negative thoughts try to push their weight around, we can bring to mind the words of Jesus to do the heavy lifting and throw them out. *Take heart!* Put another way, *have courage!* He did the fighting for us so we can enjoy the winning. The troubles we're going through are *His* to get us through. It's for our benefit that we think about what is true and good and right, because those words define our heavenly Father. He's all three of them in one and in *every* way praiseworthy.

The list goes on and on depending on the translation we read, but none of them are exaggerated. Think about whatever is noble, pure, lovely, admirable, and excellent. Fill your minds with what is reputable, authentic, gracious, beautiful, and best. The bottom line is, how we think is how we become a light for the good God we serve. What we think about makes all the difference in how we go about our lives, and how we influence the lives of others.

FATHER, LET THE TRUTH OF YOUR CHARACTER
ALWAYS BE IN THE FOREFRONT OF MY MIND,
SO THAT WHAT OTHERS SEE IN ME IS
EVERY GOOD THING IN YOU.

QUIET SPACE NEEDED

You're my place of quiet retreat;
I wait for Your word
to renew me.

PSALM 119:114 THE MESSAGE

Even before the worldwide pandemic I was a social distance proponent. I've always chosen the beach that I know is least populated, and if it *does* get crowded, I walk until I find an isolated spot. I know I'm not the only one who defines personal space as "enough area around me to avoid small talk or touching of any kind." We introverts just need more alone time than most and have a little more difficulty when we meet a hugger.

Even if we're not introverts, all of us need the place of quiet retreat that is our heavenly Father. We can read and remember every truth written, which is invaluable for our spiritual strength and well-being, but God renews us on a very *personal* level in the quiet times. It's a hard thing to explain but it's a certainty, nonetheless.

A hurricane wind ripped through the mountains and

shattered the rocks before God, but God wasn't to be found in the wind; after the wind an earthquake, but God wasn't in the earthquake; and after the earthquake fire, but God wasn't in the fire; and after the fire a gentle and quiet whisper. I KINGS 19:11-12 THE MESSAGE

God hasn't changed since Elijah heard that whisper. He wants us to get to a place away from the noise of the world so we can *listen*. Our part is to make the space in our lives to do it. When we're struggling the most, time to listen becomes most important. Our "place of quiet retreat" is also the God of the impossible, our great reward, our shield, and the One who takes hold of our right hand and says, *"Do not fear; I will help you."* Maybe today is a good day to make our getaway plan.

FATHER, GIVE ME A HEART
THAT LISTENS MORE CLOSELY,
A SOUL THAT HEARS MORE CLEARLY,
AND A SPIRIT THAT FOLLOWS YOU MORE
FAITHFULLY EVERY DAY. WHEN I'M RENEWED
BY YOUR WORD, THERE'S A NEW COURAGE
IN ME TO SERVE AND BE A LIGHT.

A LOVE MIGHTIER
THAN THE MESS

*Mightier than the thunder of
great waters, mightier than
the breakers of the sea—
the Lord on high is mighty.*

PSALM 93:4 NIV

*H*ave you ever been to the beach when a hurricane is threatening the coast? The waves sound like a continuous roll of thunder. God's eternal power is always visible in the greatness of the ocean, but when the waters are turbulent and unsettled, there's a different feeling of reverence for our almighty Creator. It's an awe-inspiring reminder that He can do *anything*. Nothing is beyond His control or capability. And it also brings an incredible peace to know He's both father and friend to us all.

Do you remember any mistakes or missteps from your past? Do you remember the spiritual growth God brought out

of them? Know what's awesome? God doesn't remember *any* of them. Where would we be if our failures were recorded the way our tears are? He doesn't do that and never would, and that truth exposes His heart so beautifully. Our lives can seem like a cluttered mess of wrong choices and failures, but we serve a God who uses messy lives to show the world how amazing His grace really is. How is it apparent in a life that's perfectly put together? He's the champion of the forgotten and a hero to the heartbroken. And the grace we have through Jesus is mightier than any mess we can possibly make of our lives.

When we start to feel guilty about the impatience that edged out a loving response today or the worry that got in the way of our peace or the frustration that became the wrong words spoken, we need to replace the shame with the mercy and grace waiting for us at the throne of grace. A place we're invited to approach with confidence. A place that reminds us of the One who rules the sea. And the Lord on high hasn't lost an ounce of His power.

FATHER, YOUR GRACE IS THE SEA
THAT DROWNS MY SHAME AND
WASHES AWAY THE MISTAKES I'VE MADE.
MY HEART IS FULL OF PRAISE AND WONDER
AT THE POWER OF YOUR LOVE.

FOCUS!

How blessed is God!
And what a blessing He is!...
Long before He laid down
earth's foundations, He had us
in mind, had settled on us as
the focus of His love.

EPHESIANS 1:3-4 THE MESSAGE

We all have things that distract us from what we should be doing. When I have a deadline to meet, I start baking. I try a cookie recipe I haven't tried before, or I throw together a batch of my favorite chocolate cupcakes. I read about authors who have quiet, secluded places to go when they have a book to finish and I wish I was one of them! I sometimes wonder why God has called me to do what I do because my attention span doesn't lend itself to the successful completion of projects *or* books. The fact that you're reading this right now is no small miracle. But God has never been one to shy away from employing the underqualified, and for that I'm profoundly grateful.

Thankfully, God doesn't have trouble focusing on the most important things. And it's both humbling and exciting that we have always been His *most important thing*. We were the focus of His love before the foundations of the earth were laid. That's *forever* stuff. There hasn't been a moment in time or before time existed that we haven't been extravagantly loved. How can we have bad days in light of that truth? I scroll through my social media feeds and see face after face and think the only thing that *any* of us truly want is to be loved. We want to be known and seen, through and through. Not in a superficial way, but in a real, deep-down way. God loves us like that. He likes us too, and if He could like every picture we post He would. He wants us to know we are *known*. We are *seen*. We are loved more than we can fully understand.

When He made us, fearfully and wonderfully so, He was completely in love. He knew we were going to be here long before we arrived, and when we did His eyes lit up with joy. You're the focus of His love today. He sees and knows every need, fear, insecurity, and hope—and because you're His most important thing, you have His full attention.

FATHER, I'M WHOLE IN YOUR PERFECT LOVE
AND THANKFUL FOR IT EVERY DAY.

MAKING TIME
TO SPEND TIME

Seek the Lord;
yes, seek His strength and
seek His face untiringly.

1 CHRONICLES 16:11 TLB

The ocean brings both evidence of and reverence for God's power and presence. There's a reason we love to go to the beach, a reason the experience restores us, a reason it's hard to be stressed out when we're there. God's existence is seen in everything He created, and oceans are one of His *biggest* created things! Have you enjoyed people watching at the beach? Everyone there seems to have this amazing positive energy. You can just see joy, peace, reflection, awe, inspiration, rest, relaxation, and smiles. There are *so* many smiles. Imagine how happy it must make God to see the beach bring all of those things to us—His *crowning* creation.

Earth's beauty is a constant reminder of God's love for us. Nature draws our hearts to Him because He designed all of

this with us in mind. There's a direct connection to Him in all of it and our spirit loves the *camaraderie*. I love the definition of that word: *A mutual trust and friendship among those who spend a lot of time together.* We need time away from the bustle of the world and our daily demands to nurture our trust and friendship with God. He's our life. He's every breath we take. He's our shelter, strength, hope, and peace. If we neglect to spend a lot of time with Him, the abundant life that Jesus came to give is lost in the rush. We have to be deliberate about disconnecting from the world to connect with our Father.

Ever wonder how exercising gives you more energy even though you are too tired to exercise in the first place? But if you discipline yourself to do it, it works. Expending energy to exercise gives you *more* energy. Likewise, we might think we just don't have *time* to spend time with God. But if we discipline ourselves to do it regularly, things start falling into place a lot more smoothly, and we feel *less* pressed—for time, patience, self-control, and all the other good things we're going to get in abundance from connecting with Him.

FATHER, GIVE ME WISDOM TO KNOW
THE BEST WAYS TO SPEND TIME WITH YOU.

HANDING IT ALL OVER

I've cultivated a quiet heart.

PSALM 131:2 THE MESSAGE

Cultivating anything takes some work. If we want our plants to grow, we have to prepare the soil correctly and continue to give them our attention until they become healthy and vibrant. In the same way, it takes time, attention, and a little work to develop a quiet heart. We don't become patient in a day. We don't trust God completely after the first time He proves how faithful He is. We don't master peacefulness and self-control without a lot of practice. And the trials of life, changing circumstances, people we meet and even *our* people give us opportunities to practice that pretty often.

When it comes to maintaining a quiet heart, practice is good and failures are inevitable—but continued success will only come through an investment in prayer. We will never get to a quiet heart without going to God. Life will keep throwing curve balls, trials will keep coming, days will keep feeling impossibly difficult, and we'll need the strength He gives to make it through. The great thing is, the more times we have to run to Him, the more peace we get to enjoy. When we throw up our hands, He grabs both of them and pulls us up again.

In exchange for surrender He fills us with a calmness we can't get anywhere else.

Learning to trust is another part of cultivating a quiet heart. Our flesh likes to hold on to some of the control. We like to think we don't need God to be involved in every little thing, why bother Him with it all? But what would happen if we *did* bother Him with every single detail? It draws us close to Him and in turn He draws close to each of us. We want God close. We want Him micromanaging our life. He's *great* with details, just study any single thing in nature and the way it's designed. Today will bring chances to cultivate a quiet heart—let's start by handing it all over to God.

FATHER, I INVITE YOU INTO EVERY MOMENT
OF MY DAY AND ASK FOR YOUR GRACE
IN THE THINGS THAT CHALLENGE MY QUIET HEART.
THANK YOU FOR BEING CLOSE, LOVING ME BEST,
AND CARING ABOUT EVERY LITTLE THING.

LEARNING FROM THE TEXTBOOK ON LOVE

Let Me teach you;
for I am gentle and humble,
and you shall find rest
for your souls.

MATTHEW 11:28 TLB

I'm starting to love cloudy beach days. I remember my first adventure to the beach during the summer. I packed my bag like I normally do with all the things I normally need. If you've ever been to a beach in a subtropical region in the middle of July, you know you need to take some things you might not "normally" take. I go alone, so I've never been in the habit of bringing a canopy or umbrella with me. I quickly discovered on that blistering July day that I was going to need a break from the heat. To my dismay it was a cloudless day. It ended up being the shortest beach day I've ever had. And I gained a new appreciation for clouds and canopies.

It's good to be a lifelong learner. There are things all along the way that teach us how to be better friends, parents, siblings, coworkers, and most importantly, people who love God and the people He made. And that includes everybody. Jesus is the best teacher of the things that matters most. Through His life on earth He left us a clear example of how to live. Still, we need to let Him teach us. We need to keep studying the words He spoke and the life He lived. It's our path to finding rest. Real rest for our souls. He's gentle and humble, so He won't force the lessons on us or make us accept the guidance He offers.

Like clouds on a sunny day give us a cool break and a little relief, learning how Jesus handled life gives us a break from the burden of trying to figure it out on our own. We're human, so we're not always going to remember how to get it right. His life is the textbook on love, and love is what we're here to do. It's a simple command, but we won't master it in a lifetime. All we can do is learn how to get better at it, but only by letting our Master teach us.

FATHER, TEACH ME TO LISTEN AND FOLLOW,
TO LOVE AND REST, TO DAILY SURRENDER
TO A LIFETIME OF LEARNING YOUR WAYS.

Solitude with God repairs the damage done by the fret and noise and clamour of the world.

—OSWALD CHAMBERS

THE DIVINE PICK-ME-UP

After you have suffered a little while, our God, who is full of kindness through Christ, will give you His eternal glory. He personally will come and pick you up, and set you firmly in place, and make you stronger than ever.

1 PETER 5:10 TLB

It's so fun to watch children at the beach. Their fearlessness of the ocean, handfuls of shells, curiosity about every bird, happiness over every dog, carelessness about how covered in sand they are—all of it is a joy to see. Children are gifts from God, and the things they teach us, if we're wise enough to pay attention, can show us a little about what the kingdom of heaven looks like. Maybe a lot.

They're innocence can walk them into danger at times, and I've seen it several times at the beach. To a child, the waves look like pure, harmless fun until they get knocked down and can't stand back up on their own. There have been a few watchful beachgoers I've seen run to rescue a child on more than one occasion. A parent turns their back for a second and their child is in trouble without them realizing it.

We fall down in life, too, but thankfully our Father *never* turns His back. Not for a moment. The trouble we face might last longer than we'd like it to or think it should, but God is full of kindness. He knows precisely when to come and pick us up, set us firmly in place, and make us stronger than ever. Coming to our rescue too soon would dilute the courage He's building in us. Coming too late might lead to resentment and giving up hope. But God knows exactly where our heart is at all times. And our heart is His priority. We've been given the faith to walk the journey of our lives victoriously. There's no doubt we'll be tempted to give up hope, but God will always provide a way out of the temptation. He knows our limits better than we do. And He's going to keep picking us up as many times as we need Him to, while making us stronger every time.

FATHER, THANK YOU FOR YOUR KINDNESS, FAITHFULNESS, AND TIMELINESS. WHEN I FACE TRIALS, I'M GROWING STRONG AND LEARNING THAT MY ONLY HOPE IS IN YOU.

OUT OF CONTROL BUT IN GOD'S HANDS

Put your hope in God and know real blessing! God made sky and soil, sea and all the fish in it. He always does what He says.

PSALM 146:6 THE MESSAGE

Coastal beaches have ever-changing landscapes. Erosion caused by waves, currents, tides, wind-driven water and storm impact creates a new view nearly year-round. Even though measures are taken to prevent the erosion, the causes are out of our control. There are many things that can change how our lives look, yet we have no control over the cause. We can't make decisions for the people we love, even though their choices directly affect us. We can't force friends to treat us with the love of God, even though their actions could affect the landscape of our relationship for a long time. We can't demand that we get the job we applied for, even though we're sure it would be the best plan for our needs.

The thing we can control is where we put our hope and trust. Like the Scripture says, *put your hope in God and know real blessing!* We may not be able to see clearly in the short term, but time will reveal the *real* blessings. The ones God sends. The ones we understand fully in hindsight. The ones that, when He lays them in our laps with perfect love and impeccable timing, bring us to our knees, and to tears of joy.

God always does what He says. Our part is to trust Him no matter *what*. No matter how dark it gets, no matter how hopeless it looks, no matter how scary it feels—God will not leave us! The blessings that make their way to us through a mountain of uncontrollable events and unbelievable circumstances are the ones we can't take a *smidgen* of credit for. One hundred percent of the glory goes right where it should. To the One who made it happen. He's working things out for us now, today, for the blessings on the way. I'm excited to see what they are, aren't you?

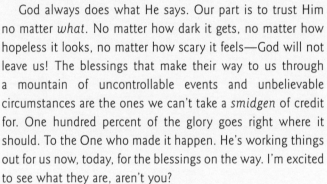

FATHER, THE BLESSINGS YOU HAVE PREPARED
ARE MORE THAN I CAN IMAGINE,
ORCHESTRATED PERFECTLY BY YOUR LOVE
AND THE UNMERITED FAVOR WE HAVE IN JESUS.
THANK YOU.

OUR LIVES ARE PENNED WITH PERFECT LOVE

Every day of my life was recorded in Your book. Every moment was laid out before a single day had passed.

PSALM 139:16 NLT

I'm grateful God wrote so many beach days into the story of my life. At the ocean I'm deeply inspired, incredibly thankful, always prayerful, and *still*. I've lived near the coast for two years, and before beach days became the norm for me, I didn't slow down very often. Writing kept me quiet and still, of course, but little else did. I found it difficult to sit still long enough to watch a movie. Like so many of us in our fast-paced lives, we get into the mindset that staying busy means we're driven, motivated, successful people. While that can prove to be true, it might be tempting us to get our priorities out of order.

I recently read that in Hebrew, the phrase "be still" in Psalm 46 means to "let go or to release." Along with being still, giving up control is another hard one for a lot of us. But fear and anxiety are the other two peas in the pod with control. The three of them go together, and none of them are good for us. The Psalm is essentially saying, "let go and know God is in control." Because we belong to Him, we don't have to be afraid. Every moment of our lives was laid out before a single day passed. And God is *always* good. He writes beauty and purpose into every one of our stories.

When we feel like our lives are speeding up and our days are spinning slightly out of control, it's time to sit still for a minute, take a deep breath, and let go. Release the stress, the doubt, the fear, and turn it over to God. We aren't going to be able to manage everything perfectly, and thankfully we don't have to. We have a Father whose perfect love is in control of our lives. Every moment that's written was penned with that love and it will never fade—no matter how many times we try to take the pen out of His hand.

FATHER, I KNOW I CAN'T DO THIS WITHOUT YOU.
MY LIFE IS IN YOU. GIVE ME THE COURAGE
TO LIVE IT COMPLETELY SURRENDERED EVERY DAY.

MORE-THAN-ENOUGH
THROUGH ME

*Now glory be to God,
who by His mighty power at work
within us is able to do far more
than we would ever dare to ask
or even dream of—infinitely
beyond our highest prayers,
desires, thoughts, or hopes.*

EPHESIANS 3:20 TLB

We serve a God of more than. More than enough. More than we expected. More than we would ever dare to ask for or even dream of. Why is God so generous to us? Could it be to give us a small idea of the magnitude of His love? Or the slightest inkling of the vastness of His grace? Both more than we will ever wrap our minds around. And yet, we've been

given His love and grace freely, never having to earn a single drop of either one.

Somewhere between the time we're very young and the time we become a teenager, we adopt the belief that we have to please the people around us to be loved, appreciated, and accepted. It's not true, and it's a horrible feeling. The pressure that social media puts on kids today is heartbreaking. There have been several tragic stories that have come from the lies it feeds and perpetuates. But God has a dream for all of us. It was woven into our being with love, beauty, and purpose. Not one of us is here to prove to anyone that we're lovable. We're loved without condition and without boundaries.

It's hard to keep that in the forefront of our minds all the time. We carry a computer in our hand everywhere we go, giving us access to the temptations of comparison, competition, and a false sense of "company." We spend too much time looking down and not enough time lifting people up. We've all been walking through some rough waters, but God is at work within us. He's powering us up to be a witness to His love like never before. We have the opportunity every day to put everything aside and simply love the people in our lives—with the more-than-enough measure that God uses.

FATHER, INCREASE MY CAPACITY TO LOVE TODAY.
LET ME BE THE ONE TO SHOW OTHERS HOW
GENEROUS YOU ARE WITH EVERY HOPE THEY HAVE.

A QUIET LIFE

*In repentance and rest
is your salvation, in quietness
and trust is your strength.*

ISAIAH 30:15 NIV

One of the last sweet memories I have with my dad is a walk on the beach. He spent his life in construction, so he loved seeing the beautiful houses that were built along the oceanfront. One in particular was a stately mansion that begged you to stop and look. Coincidentally, we were walking past a gentleman who knew the story of the house, and when he saw us admiring it, he stopped to share. A businessman had the house built for his wife, but they were rarely there. How sad, I thought. Such a grand gesture left empty and underappreciated. The structure was magnificent, but the heart of it was lifeless. Dad and I thought the same thing—it looks great on the outside but there's nothing on the inside, the way our lives should never be.

My dad was a quiet man. He built a lot of houses in his lifetime, but the greatest thing he built was an unshakeable trust in God. We learned by his example that faith was the foundation of a good life and Jesus was the cornerstone of an eternal one. I'm thankful for the gift of his life. We don't know all the ways our lives will influence the people around us, but my dad is proof that we don't have to be loud about it. Living a quiet life is encouraged over and over in Scripture, and I believe it's because faith and love are more about what we do than what we say.

If our hearts are secure in our salvation and trusting God completely, the life inside us will manifest outwardly in acts of kindness, generosity, and selflessness. At my dad's wake we found out there were some things he had graciously done for people that we had no idea about. I saw him buy groceries for families, sacrifice his time, take the coat off his back and give it away, and countless other small reflections of Jesus, but he had quietly done so much more. I hope we find ways to love quietly today, because that's the best way to speak volumes about the God we serve.

FATHER, LET ME BE A VESSEL
OF YOUR LOVE TO THE PEOPLE IN MY LIFE
AND THOSE YOU BRING INTO IT.

OCEANIC LOVE FOR EVERY LITTLE THING

God's love is meteoric, His loyalty
astronomic, His purpose titanic,
His verdicts oceanic. Yet in
His largeness nothing gets lost;
Not a man, not a mouse,
slips through the cracks.

PSALM 36:5-6 THE MESSAGE

Standing at the ocean makes us feel small. It's overwhelming at times to know that the One who created it, pooled it and is keeping it in place is watching over every detail of every living thing on earth. Down to the lowly sparrow. Is it possible because His life is in every breath taken? It's amazing to think about and too profound to comprehend. At the same time, it's the most comforting assurance Jesus gave us. He told us the

Father knows when a sparrow falls, and if that isn't enough to realize your worth to Him, He also knows the number of hairs on your head. These truths seem impossible in our finite thinking.

To be sure, God is paying *close* attention. When we think He can't possibly know or care about this little problem we're facing today, or that He's overlooked us because, let's face it, there are far more serious things happening all over the world, we're just flat-out *wrong*. He sees. And because His love for us couldn't be measured if we emptied every ocean drop-by-drop, He cares with every inch of His gigantic, Father's heart. He knows that when He shows up in the tiniest details, it makes us even braver for the big things.

Let's start the day by taking every little thing to Him while we have our morning coffee. What's our day look like? Are there things we're a little anxious about? Is there stuff we need a little wisdom to tackle? Will there be unexpected things He already knows about that we'll need a little courage to handle? God is ready to pour His love into every little part of our day. Nothing is going to slip through the cracks—and everything is going to be okay.

FATHER, I'M LAYING THE LITTLE THINGS
AT YOUR FEET TODAY AND LETTING YOUR LOVE
COVER ME AND CARRY ME THROUGH.

LOVE'S UNIQUE EXPRESSIONS

Let every created thing
give praise to the Lord,
for He issued His command,
and they came into being.

PSALM 148:5 NLT

When I found my first unbroken sand dollar on the beach, I was excited. Finding them intact is rare. I had just made a significant move, both physically and relationally, and I saw it as a tiny love note from God to say, "*you're right where you belong.*" The legend tied to the sand dollar is widely known, and I find it inspiring because the skeleton of this sea urchin truly *is* a remarkable reflection of God's hand in every created detail. I don't know if it's possible to look at an ocean, a starry sky, a mountain range, or a bumblebee pollenating a flower and keep our hearts from swelling with praise.

God created each of us to reflect Him in a unique way.

The ways I express my love for Him and His love for others is going to be different than the ways you do. One is not better than the other, they're simply not the same because *we're* not the same. Love doesn't need to act identically; it just needs to *act*. I like to write personal notes, bake, cook, help the sweet elderly woman who's at the store by herself, be the driver letting too many cars cut in, etc., etc. My list of ways to say "*I love God and God loves you*" is unique to the way I'm knit together—and your list is tied perfectly to the uniqueness of your purpose and personality.

We're in this world together and we're here to get *really* good at loving God and loving each other. That's all. It's not more complicated than that. The way to infuse love into all we do is to keep our hearts close to the One who *is* love. For me, falling in love with God every day means seeing Him in everything: the good things, the trying things, the impossibly difficult things. Love grows stronger and deeper when we go through tough times, and I want my love for God to be strong and deep. It'll make the love I give away even brighter.

FATHER, SHOW ME ALL THE WAYS
I CAN SHOW LOVE TODAY.
OPEN MY EYES TO EVERY CHANCE YOU GIVE,
SO OTHERS SEE YOU.

PUTTING LOVE
IN ITS PLACE

*He has shaped each person
in turn; now He watches
everything we do.*

PSALM 33:15 THE MESSAGE

God doesn't compare us to one another, nor does He have favorites. We're human. We do that. God shaped each of us with perfect love, at the perfect time, and gave each of us a perfectly fitting purpose. It's hard to knock down the tendency we have to compare ourselves to others, wondering if we're as good, as qualified, as smart, or as successful. When we do that, we're putting things that don't matter as much in the way of things that matter *most*. If we want to think of life as a competition, which it isn't, we should try to be the #1 kindest person on the planet. We should try to beat everyone to the finish line of forgiveness. We should try to win the championship ribbon for "most deeds completed with love."

God is watching everything we do and when He looks at

the stack of things I've been up to, I hope what He sees is a pile of love. I hope my actions remind Him of things He would do. No matter how far we climb up the ladder in life, it isn't going to get us any closer to our Father. We draw close to Him and He draws close to us through the very thing that He *is*. Love. It's what we're created by and it's what we're created for.

If there's a need that pops up today and our hearts feel a tug in love's direction, I pray we drop what we're doing and run toward it with our arms open wide. So many things can wait, but love isn't one of them. Life is fragile and love should never be put on hold. Right now is always the right time to be the love of God in this world. We *all* win when that happens.

FATHER, LET LOVE BE THE PRIORITY OF
MY DAY AND THE MOTIVATION OF MY HEART
AS I SURRENDER MY TIME TO YOU.
HELP ME SEE THE NEEDS AND BE THE SERVANT.

*Thank the
miracle-working God...
the God who laid out
earth on ocean foundations.
His love never quits.*

PSALM 136:4–5 THE MESSAGE

NO MATTER WHAT
AND BEYOND

We are able to hold our heads high no matter what happens and know that all is well, for we know how dearly God loves us.

ROMANS 5:5 TLB

I woke up and opened the blinds to a beautiful sunrise. The morning coastal showers were past and the sky was clearing. My plan to go to the beach was looking good. The temperature was perfect, the sky was blue, and the sun was shining as I drove to my favorite spot. I reached the walkway to the beach and thought the wind was a little stronger than usual, but not too out of the norm. Until I got all unpacked and settled into my chair. The first time the sand blew across my face, I didn't think much of it. I smiled and thought, natural exfoliation! Then it happened a couple more times. I started noticing people leaving shortly after arriving. The one thing *I couldn't see*—the thing I *had no wisdom about*—was the fact that when the wind is from a certain direction at a certain speed, sitting in the sand isn't a great way to spend the day. It was a rookie beachgoing mistake, but it was a mistake, nonetheless.

There are times when we make a decision and expect a great result. There are no giant red flags or glitches that keep us from following through. All the markers look good. By all appearances, everything is going to turn out as planned. And then it doesn't. Thankfully, *no matter what happens we can know that all is well because we know how dearly God loves us*. The thing we hope to get better at is making sure we ask the One who *can* see all things, has all the wisdom and freely offers it to anyone who asks, and oh-by-the-way, has already gone ahead of us.

I would've been wise to watch the weather report that morning before going to the beach, but everything *seemed* so perfect I went ahead and decided on my own. God loves us and uses our mistakes to lovingly teach us and make us wiser, which is why even our falls prove beneficial. We can stand back up stronger, braver, and believing with more certainty that God loves us beyond the universe and back again.

FATHER, THANK YOU FOR LOVING ME BIG!

POWERING UP TO STAY STRONG

I am with you;
that is all you need.
My power shows up best
in weak people.

2 CORINTHIANS 12:9 TLB

A solo walk on the beach early in the morning, before the crowds, the dogs, the frisbees, and the surfers take over, is one of the most peaceful, therapeutic things for the soul. And it never feels like you're isolated or alone. God is so magnificently present in the breathtaking view of the ocean, the sky, the lap of every wave, the poetry of the pelican's wings as they glide just above the water's surface. It fills your heart full with contentment. Everything is a reminder of His promise—*I am with you. That is all you need.*

When we get weary from lists, laundry, lines, long days, listening to the news, and the litany of little things that test

our patience every day, the only way to power through is to pray God's power shows up. Without fail it'll come, and we'll realize again we can't do this alone. We weren't created to go it alone, so feeling tired and weak is a good reminder. God loves to reenergize us for the faith race we're in, and He's cheering us on too, because we're running straight to Him.

It's one thing to feel spent physically but another to feel worn out spiritually. They're directly connected, which is why it's so important to go to God for regular fill-ups. Renewing our minds with the truth, recounting the way Jesus depended on God to fulfill His purpose, and replacing any self-sufficient tendencies with an all-sufficient God, *that's* how we tap into the power we need. When we start accomplishing things we aren't really qualified to do and handling life with a spirit of joy when our circumstances should make us anything but joyful, we become a billboard for God's power in us. Yes, we're weak, but it only magnifies the strength we depend on. We want God to keep shining through us and dimming down our idea that we can handle our lives without Him. He's not just part of what we need, He's *all* we need.

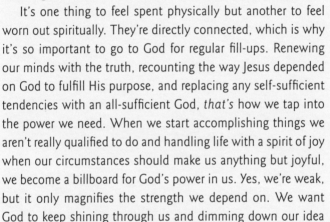

FATHER, I'M THANKFUL FOR THE STRENGTH
YOU GIVE WHEN I NEED IT MOST.
I WANT TO BE AWARE OF MY DEPENDENCE
ON YOU DAILY.

LETTING LOVE LEAD

*His love is
the wonder of the world.*

PSALM 31:22 THE MESSAGE

I have a friend whose eighteen-month-old granddaughter loves the beach. On her first visit she ran carefree and confidently to the ocean when she saw it. When they walk the shore together, her little hand can barely reach his to hold on, but she stretches up and holds on. Living without cares and holding on tightly sounds like the way we should be walking with God every day! His love is bigger than the oceans combined. His mercy stretches from east to west and His thoughts of us outnumber the grains of sand. His goodness outshines the sun and every star in the heavens. His love is the wonder of the world and the purpose of our being.

"*What a stack of blessing You have piled up for those who worship You, ready and waiting for all who run to you to escape an unkind world. You hide them safely away.*" That's what comes earlier in Psalm 31. Like a child who runs to the ocean without an ounce of worry, God waits for us to run to Him without an any hesitation. He's a refuge from the unkind world we live in. He's our hiding place from the harshness of pain, disappointment, and the daily grind. When we run to Him there's never criticism or condemnation. Instead, there's comfort and compassion. We don't get a recap of the mistakes we made today or a lecture on how we can do better tomorrow. We get smothered in love. We get piles of grace. We get stacks of reasons we should keep on hoping.

God is the best way to have the best day. He wants to be involved from start to finish. He wants us to reach up and hold onto His hand so He can lead. He knows where He needs us to be, who He needs us to talk to, and what He needs us to do. Let's stay flexible and follow with open hearts and a joyful willingness—He's ready to bring the blessings so we can be a blessing!

FATHER, I WANT TO BE WILLING
TO CHANGE MY PLANS FOR YOUR PURPOSE.
GIVE ME A HEART THAT LETS YOUR LOVE LEAD.

A CLEAN HEART
FOR A BRIGHT LIFE

Create in me a new,
clean heart, O God. Renew
a loyal spirit within me.

PSALM 51:10 NLT

There's a wonderful group of volunteers who work to keep the shoreline litter free and clear of things that could be harmful to coastal wildlife. Their diligence restores the natural beauty of the beach and makes it pleasant for everyone to enjoy. Have you ever wondered what it would look like if they didn't offer to do such a good and generous thing? In time, the clutter would make a typically beautiful place ugly and unappealing. It would be sad if our beaches were left unkept. It would diminish the splendor of one of the most magnificent gifts in God's creation.

The beauty of our lives can become dulled, too, if we don't invite God to "create in us a new, clean heart." Our heart can be many things. Humble and contrite or proud

and arrogant. Hardened by rejection, shame, and sin, or soft and pliable in the hands of a loving God. Asking God to sweep our heart clean and renew our spirit is something we should do faithfully. The world and its distractions can make a mess of what grace made spotless. Spiritual maintenance keeps our life in the best possible shape for God to use— and we want usable, surrendered lives that make everyone want to meet Him. He's always welcoming, always safe, and always beautiful.

To wake up and know we've been chosen to shine God's light in this world should make us excited about every sunrise. We should be thrilled about being loyal servants of the King of kings, and we should look forward to showing everyone what He's like. He's the heart-shaper who uses love, kindness, compassion, patience, gentleness and hope to clean out whatever has caused our hearts to believe *anything* other than the truth that we are fearfully and wonderfully made, and His works are *marvelous*. You're a one-of-a-kind miracle, and God wrote some things into your day that only you can do. His design is flawless—and you are *priceless*.

FATHER, CLEANSE MY HEART FOR YOUR GLORY
AND THE THINGS YOU'VE CREATED ME TO DO.
GIVE ME COURAGE TO BURY THE LIES
MY HEART BELIEVES WITH THE TRUTH OF
YOUR INCREDIBLE LOVE AND GRACE.

LOVE IN EVERY DROP

He has showered down upon us
the richness of His grace—
for how well He understands
us and knows what is best
for us at all times.

EPHESIANS 1:8 TLB

I had been on the beach for most of the day when the rain clouds started building off the coast. I checked to make sure there was no dangerous lightning in them and decided to sit it out. The afternoon showers pass quickly. I sat in my chair as the raindrops started to fall, gradually becoming a perfectly refreshing shower. I smiled while I watched a father and son continue throwing their football, shell seekers keep collecting, and friends walk along the shore talking and laughing. Within a few minutes the rain stopped, and the sun was out again in full glory.

This day at the beach wasn't the first time I'd sat silently watching a rain shower and likened it to God's goodness. It's a beautiful picture of grace. Grace that washes over us with the forgiveness we don't deserve and the favor we didn't earn. It's overwhelming to think about. Every step of getting to the grace we're given was motivated by love. God's only son leaving His side to walk in humanity's shoes, suffer more than we'll ever have to, and die a cruel death to face the fight for eternal life—and *win* it. All driven by the love of our Father, who refused to leave us stranded in sin.

It's impossible to count the drops in a rain shower, and it's impossible to put a number on the blessings we're given in a lifetime. Even in a *day*. The meter is ticking every time we take a breath, every time the sun comes up, and every time we stumble and need to draw a little more from the bottomless pool of His amazing grace. Watching the raindrops fall is a good way to reflect for a moment on the *countless* times we're forgiven, times we're strengthened, times we go to God for hope, courage, and love that never runs dry. Enjoy the showers He sends your way today, and let them refresh you with the eternal love in every single drop.

FATHER, MY HEART IS THANKFUL
FOR GRACE AND EVERYTHING IT BRINGS—
YOUR GENEROUS FAVOR, YOUR TENDER
FORGIVENESS, YOUR PERFECT PEACE,
AND YOUR UNCONDITIONAL LOVE.

OCEAN AIR AND
A HAPPY HEART

Be happy. Grow in Christ....
Live in harmony and peace.

II CORINTHIANS 13:11 TLB

*O*cean air has health benefits. As it turns out, it has happy-making benefits too. There are negative ions in sea air which speed up our ability to absorb oxygen and balance serotonin levels. Serotonin is the key hormone that stabilizes our mood, feelings of well-being, and happiness. No wonder we feel more alert, relaxed, and energized after a day at the beach! Have you ever been on the beach when a pre-school visited? The children come running down the pathway with their brightly colored matching t-shirts and shell bags in hand. Their faces are filled with so much curiosity and delight you can't help catching some of it.

It would be great if we could bottle up a child's delight and pour a little on our attitude every day. If we could open our eyes and be happy for the gift of life and excited about discovering *one* more way to grow in love and get better at

things like forgiveness, patience, kindness, and compassion. It's something to stay curious about, the endless riches we have in Jesus. In our lifetime we won't understand the magnitude of it all, but the lovely surprises along the journey should make us run toward Him every day with a big smile on our face.

There will be hard things God allows that will be even harder to understand. But He holds us close through those times and sees our heart in the end. Strengthened, yet softer. Broken, yet braver. Challenged, yet changed for His glory. We can always trust the choices of His love. If we look for His love in every circumstance and keep our "shell bags" in hand, we can pick up the gems of wisdom, the pieces of beauty, and all the broken things He fills with light. And we can keep on trusting Him to help us grow in grace until we see Him face to face.

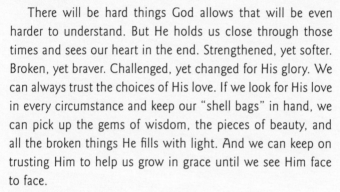

FATHER, WHEN I TRUST YOU,
I LEARN TO SEE YOUR PERFECT LOVE IN
EVERYTHING. I ASK YOU FOR THE COURAGE
TO KEEP GROWING, ESPECIALLY THROUGH
THE THINGS THAT ARE HARD ON MY HEART
AND NOT EASY TO UNDERSTAND.

GETTING BETTER AT CHOOSING BETTER

Be generous with your lives. By opening up to others, you'll prompt people to open up with God, this generous Father in heaven.

MATTHEW 5:16 THE MESSAGE

I'm not good at just *being* with people. I'm the one at the dinner table jumping up every couple of minutes to fill glasses, tidy up, make sure everyone has enough to eat, and so on. I've missed long stretches of conversations because I thought I better start loading the dishwasher or washing the pans. I've always struggled with the idea of *being* over *doing*. It's hard for me to open up to others too—but I'm hoping God's strength is showing up a little more every day in my weakness. I've missed too many opportunities to genuinely connect with people, even those closest to me. In an attempt to justify my busyness, I've thrown down the "*I'm the servant type*" card. But then, *the story*.

I can relate to the story about Mary and Martha in a personal way. My sister Becky is a warm, lovable, extrovert who loves *being* with people. She sits so beautifully, and is inspiringly generous with her life. She's open and vulnerable, and the love of God in her has prompted countless people to *"open up with God, our generous Father in heaven."* I think you can see who's who in *our* story. I can almost hear Jesus saying, *"Bonnie, Bonnie...."*

God's design of every single life He creates is flawless. We're wonderfully unique. The design is divine and the purpose is perfect, but we're all imperfect *people* in desperate need of our Savior. We need Him every day. We need Him to show us how to choose like Mary did—what is better, *so it won't be taken away from us*. The investments we make in *relationships* are the things that make it to eternity. He's a caring, loving Father who wants a personal relationship with each one of us. If we open our hearts and lives enough to be vulnerable with people, His love will shine through our imperfections and right into their need. They'll see the love that will not only save them, but heal, comfort, and accept them like never before.

FATHER, YOUR STRENGTH IS MADE PERFECT IN MY WEAKNESS. YOUR LOVE IS CLEARER THROUGH MY WILLINGNESS. HELP ME BE OPEN AND VULNERABLE MORE OFTEN, COURAGEOUSLY AND UNAFRAID.

GOD REDEEMS AND CHAMPIONS EVERYTHING (GRACE)

So we're not giving up. How could we! Even though on the outside it often looks like things are falling apart on us, on the inside, where God is making new life, not a day goes by without His unfolding grace.

II CORINTHIANS 4:16-17 THE MESSAGE

We're going to have them! Gray days, hard-to-get-out-of-bed days, and days when everything that can go wrong, *does*. For those days we crawl into the arms of *grace*, being sure that God Redeems And Champions Everything. He doesn't take vacation days from our lives. He's with us even when it looks like He can't possibly be. When we've prayed, cried, hoped, thanked, and put both hands in the air in surrender, and find our aching heart still saying, "Where *is* He?"

He's working on a great story of *redemption*—smack dab in the middle of whatever trial *seems* to be winning. He's championing every single detail that leads to the best, brightest, *more-than-we-could-hope-for* outcome. Hard days are no match for the grace sustaining our hope. Disappointments can't dim the grace lighting our way. Barren seasons can't blind us to the grace that's creating new life on the inside of us. A life lived with unshakable confidence in God's sufficiency and faithfulness. He's got us no matter *what* is falling apart around us.

Grace unfolds as we need it. It's adequate to carry us *right now*. We don't have to think about what tomorrow will bring because God is already there, and His grace is already enough. The next time our day looks daunting and the problems look impossible and the trial appears to have no end, God is redeeming and championing *everything*. Trust Him! There isn't anything He won't do for you because He loves you more than words will ever be able to define. He gave His whole heart *to* you and *for* you in the life of His son. You are loved, heard, held, and priceless. And *nothing* can separate you from that universe-sized love or the One giving it.

FATHER, EVEN WHEN THINGS LOOK DARK AND
IMPOSSIBLE, I KNOW YOUR LOVE IS BRIGHT
AND UNSTOPPABLE. I TRUST YOU'RE WORKING
EVERYTHING TOGETHER FOR GOOD.

WE ARE TO TAKE EVERYTHING TO GOD—LITTLE THINGS, VERY LITTLE THINGS, EVEN WHAT THE WORLD CALLS TRIVIAL THINGS.

—GEORGE MUELLER

OVER AND OVER
TO GET BETTER
AND BETTER

Behold, I will do a new thing,
now it shall spring forth; shall
you not know it? I will even
make a road in the wilderness
and rivers in the desert.

ISAIAH 43:19 NKJV

Have you ever watched beginning surfers at the beach? Their determination after failing time after time is admirable and inspiring. Sometimes there's an instructor teaching them the basics, sometimes a parent, and sometimes it's just a group of friends with a few who are clearly well-seasoned in the sport. It's never on days when the big waves are there attracting experienced surfers from near and far. Beginners come on small wave days. It wouldn't be wise or practical for surfers who aren't ready to handle more difficult conditions to try putting themselves in danger or getting into situations they're unprepared for.

When we face trials of many kinds, God is preparing us. Our challenges are not without a purpose. He knows there are greater things ahead for us and for the greater good of the lives we'll touch. Our hearts are being readied. Things that build our faith are building our confidence and trust in Him for bigger waves and bigger days. Until we meet our heavenly Father face to face, we have three things to try over and over again until we get better and better at them: "Trust steadily in God, hope unswervingly, and love extravagantly. And the best of the three is love" (I CORINTHIANS 13:13 THE MESSAGE).

We have to be determined to get good at the things God has called us all to do. No matter how many times we fall, no matter how many times our plans flip upside down, no matter how many times it feels like we're going under, we have to get back up and keep trying. God is constantly guiding our lives. When it looks like going forward is impossible, we can *never give up hope* that He's making roads in the wilderness and rivers in the desert.

FATHER, I'M GRATEFUL FOR THE TRIALS AND TESTS PREPARING MY HEART TO BE BETTER AND BETTER AT BEING YOUR LOVE IN THIS WORLD. GIVE ME COURAGE TO KEEP TRUSTING, HOPING, AND STANDING ON TRUTH.

MORE THAN ENOUGH TO PRESS ON

Quiet down before God, be prayerful before Him.

PSALM 37:7 THE MESSAGE

When I introduced running to my daily routine 12 years ago, I discovered my body wanted to give up shortly after I started, usually within the first mile. I soon found out the second mile wasn't all that easy either. It was when I got to the point of making it past a third mile that I started saying to my body, "Okay, it's time to relax into your run." To my astonishment it listened. I made up my mind I wasn't going to quit and to my relief my body eventually fell in line.

Faith works a little bit the same way. When we make up our mind we're not going to give up on God, things start to fall in line. The pieces of our life start to fall into place. When we learn to relax, quiet down, and be prayerful, it gets easier to go the distance when circumstances get hard. God is faithfully setting the course of our life's marathon, and He's also the one holding out a glass of water and cheering us on

to the finish line. Drinking the water He offers will get us there with a win, and we won't be thirsty from all the running. Jesus will be there with the eternal rewards of a life lived in Him.

When we get worn out and want to give up, our living water is all the refreshment we need. He'll quiet the thoughts that tell us to stop hoping and give us the strength to keep our eyes on Him, the author and finisher of our faith. Jesus is proof that love has the power to carry us to the finish. God's love will always pull us through. *Anything*. It doesn't matter if the course ahead is uphill, we're out of breath, and we're depleted of the energy to be brave—God's unfailing, unconditional, unrelenting love is all we need. If we stay close to Him today, we can draw as much love as it takes to press on. There's more than enough for all of us, and our Father is more than willing to give it.

FATHER, YOUR LOVE GIVES ME STRENGTH
TO GO ON WHEN I WANT TO GIVE UP.
YOU ARE THE STRENGTH OF MY HEART
AND MY PORTION FOREVER.

CARRIED THROUGH
THE COURSE

Wait passionately for God,
don't leave the path.

PSALM 37:34 THE MESSAGE

I like to go barefoot as soon as I get to the beach. I don't like how flip-flops flip copious amounts of sand onto the back of my legs in the short distance from my car to my beach chair. I've had to relinquish this routine a few times. In the hotter months the sun-drenched path to the beach gets really, *really* hot. As soon as I realized the bottoms of my feet were losing layers of skin, I dropped my usual plan quickly, put on my flip-flops, and let the sand fly.

We're going to go through seasons when it'll be tough to walk the path God puts us on. We'll be faithfully doing the right things and going the right way but staying the course will be harder than we expected or feel we can endure. But endure we *will*. We'll wait patiently while God does His perfect work in us, taking our faith to a new level, teaching our hearts to trust more deeply, and helping us learn to practice the secret of contentment Paul discovered. It can't matter how uncomfortable it gets, how much we do or don't have, or how we *feel* when it comes down to taking up the cross.

When the going gets rough we get to choose to let God carry us. That choice brings far more relief than a pair of flip-flops in the hot sand and being close to His heart brings a kind of rest a day at the beach never will. When we trust Him completely and *relax* in the cradle of His arms, we find out it's a good idea to depend on Him every day, not just when the path of His will gets hard to follow. God's plan and purpose for our lives will lead to more good things than trying to go it alone ever will. His will is His word, and it's the way to the abundant life Jesus lived and died for. "I came so they can have real and eternal life, more and better life than they ever dreamed of." (JOHN 10:10 THE MESSAGE).

FATHER, KEEP MY FEET
ON THE PATH OF ABUNDANT LIFE.
I PUT ALL MY HOPE AND TRUST IN YOU.

GIVING LIFE OUR
FEARLESS ALL

We can serve God without fear,
in holiness and righteousness
for as long as we live.

LUKE 1:74-75 NLT

On a beautiful day of inspiration for this book, I sat in my beach chair and watched a father with his two young girls as they played on surfboards and swam nearly non-stop. They were with a larger group who ordered pizza and had it delivered at one point, which I thought was a pretty fun idea. My favorite part was being an audience to the *fearlessness* of these girls when they'd run and dive into the ocean. No hesitation, no intimidation from the waves, no worries when they got knocked down. Right back up they'd come to wipe their face and get back to running and diving. I'm sure their courage was undaunted because there wasn't a moment when their dad wasn't standing close by, watching carefully.

I thought to myself more than one time how amazing

it would be to *live* that way. To dive into ideas without hesitation, to not be intimidated by past failures, to stand right back up when we fall down, brush off the rejection, mistake, or disappointment and keep on living with an unquenchable, *contagious* joy. The world would notice that kind of spirited living, and they'd want to know how we do it. The answer would be simple. *My Father is always with me and He's watching carefully.*

We don't have to live afraid. God is the best Father, the kindest friend, and the truest love we will *ever* know. He's the solid foundation of our dreams, the sure source of our hope in seeing those dreams come true, and the One cheering the loudest when they do. He's all we need to live a life of fearlessness and unbridled joy. In the words of the popular hymn "His Eye Is on the Sparrow:" "Why do I feel discouraged? Why do the shadows come?... When Jesus is my portion, a constant friend is He. His eye is on the sparrow, And I know He watches me." We don't need any more than that to make today worth running into—heart first, hope secure, and joy unleashed!

FATHER, FILL MY HEART WITH FEARLESSNESS AND JOY. MAKE MY LIFE A SPOTLIGHT THAT SHINES ON YOU. GIVE ME HOPE THAT INSPIRES OTHERS TO SEE YOUR FAITHFULNESS AND KNOW YOUR LOVE.

THE UNCHANGING LOVE IN OUR EVER-CHANGING WORLD

My God is changeless
in His love for me.

PSALM 59:10 TLB

We live in a world where things change *constantly*. High and low tides change with the moon's gravitational pull on earth. The sun rises and sets at different times every day. Seasons, weather patterns, and landscapes change. On a personal level, our moods, circumstances, and relationships change. We find ourselves having to adjust to changes that are welcome and some that are not so welcome. The only way we can remain unshaken in our ever-changing lives is by being constantly aware of God's unchanging character and changeless love. Not a *single* thing can move us off the mark of His remarkable love.

> *Nothing can ever separate us from His love. Death can't, and life can't. The angels won't, and all the*

powers of hell itself cannot keep God's love away. Our fears for today, our worries about tomorrow, or where we are—high above the sky, or in the deepest ocean— nothing will ever be able to separate us from the love of God demonstrated by our Lord Jesus Christ when he died for us. ROMANS 8:38-39 TLB

That's *seriously immovable* love. God likes to show up in our lives to show how constant His love is. Love looks like the time He made something happen for us that couldn't be explained by anything other than His miracle-working hand. Love is the light in our children's eyes, shining on the truth that they're a priceless gift. Love is the pang in our heart when we see someone in need and know God has given us the way to meet it. Love is the kindness of a neighbor or friend that comes at the perfect time in the best way. God's love is the only thing that changes *lives* in a world that seems like it's moving in the wrong direction.

Let's change our day in a God way. Has our heart been nudging us to do a kindness for someone that we haven't done yet? Is there someone we can show a little more patience with, or a situation we can be more understanding about? It doesn't have to be a big thing to make the love of God shine in a big way.

FATHER, I WANT MY HANDS, HEART,
RESOURCES, AND LIFE TO BE MOVED
BY YOUR CHANGELESS LOVE.

SEEING GOD'S HAND IN A DIFFERENT WAY

I am holding you
by your right hand...
don't be afraid;
I am here to help you.

ISAIAH 41:13 TLB

Do you notice all the handholding at the beach? Elderly couples offer each other support. Dads and moms keep their little ones safe. Young couples express their budding romance. Good friends make good memories. Holding hands is a heartwarming gesture that keeps us feeling connected, safe, and loved on life's journey. We're not wired to walk it alone and because we belong to God we never have to.

When God says He's holding us by our right hand, it means He's present in our need *right now*. He's here to strengthen and help us. Like the loving Father that He is, He encourages us further with *don't be afraid*. To reiterate, *I've got you by*

the hand and I'm not going anywhere. How can we feel held by a Father we can't physically see or touch? What if we started seeing Him in other ways? The next time you catch the beauty of a butterfly in flight, think, "God is going to do a brand-new thing. See, He's already begun!" (ISAIAH 43:19); or when hundreds of sparrows come and go at your bird feeder, be reminded, "Not one sparrow...can fall to the ground without your Father knowing it" (MATTHEW 10:29) and "Look at the birds of the air; they don't sow or reap or store away in barns, and yet your heavenly Father feeds them. Are you not much more valuable than they?" (MATTHEW 6:26).

The life in His Word comes to life all around us. We just have to sharpen our spiritual eyesight and keep our minds and hearts filled with truth. We need to be so filled with the Father's promises that lies get crowded out completely. Lies like, "No one cares about you." "You're all alone in this world." "You have nothing to put your hope in." The rejoicing of our heart is knowing not *one* of these is true. Spend a little time today opening your eyes in a different way—the Father is holding your hand and has some things He'd love for you to see.

**FATHER, I KNOW YOU'RE HERE
TO STRENGTHEN ME AND NO MATTER HOW I FEEL,
I'M NEVER ALONE.**

THE BEST REWARD FOR THE BROKEN THINGS

Can you fathom the mysteries of God? Can you probe the limits of the Almighty? They are higher than the heavens above....They are deeper than the depths below.... Their measure is longer than the earth and wider than the sea.

JOB 11:7-9 NIV

When I made a long distance move for my job several years ago my daughters were devastated. Two of them were actively involved in sports, marching band, and cheerleading, and one had a high school sweetheart. It was one of the hardest things I've experienced as a parent. I cried with them, listened, and held them through their pain, trying to do everything I could as a mother to heal their broken hearts and walk them through the transition.

At my job I found a heart of wisdom who told me to ask the girls to write a letter to themselves, seal it, and read it five years after their difficult, life-changing event. In the letter they wrote down how they were feeling, what their biggest fears were, and why they thought it was the worst possible thing God could have allowed to happen. At the time they couldn't know, but before those five years had gone by they had established lifelong friendships they still enjoy, they joined a youth group they loved, and saw clearly how they had grown stronger in ways they couldn't count or fully express. They would tell you today it was one of the best seasons of their lives, but at the time, it felt unredeemable.

God leaves *nothing* in our lives unredeemed. The things He allows can feel confusing and unfair, but in perfect timing, the joy is coming. He'll lovingly pick up the scattered pieces of our broken hearts and redeem every one of them for His glory. Our gifts will be strength, wisdom, and most importantly more of *Him*. God is the greatest reward of every redemption story. He's at the center of our best life, and surrendering to Him with all our heart, mind, and soul will lead to knowing His love like never before. When we feel like everything is going wrong, He's righting everything in the most beautiful ways, from the unfathomable depths of His eternal love.

FATHER, YOUR LOVE GUIDES ME TO A LIFE FILLED WITH PURPOSE FOR YOUR GLORY. ALL I AM IS ALL YOURS, THANK YOU FOR CHOOSING ME.

LOVE SEES THE GOOD

The earth and every good thing
in it belongs to the Lord
and is yours to enjoy.

I CORINTHIANS 10:26 TLB

My youngest daughter doesn't share my love of birds. She adores elephants, but the farther away from her a bird stays, the happier she is. And she has a special disdain for seagulls. Especially when she's relaxing in her beach chair and I pull out my snack stash. The seagulls must have amazing eyesight, hearing, and intuition. They seem to know when I'm *thinking* about grabbing a snack, and as soon as I start rustling through my bag, they all come running toward us. *Swooping* and running. At which point my daughter and I agree. Seagulls are *not* on our list of "good things in the earth" for us to enjoy. I'm sure there are gull lovers out there, we just aren't among them.

I'm thankful the earth and every good thing in it belongs to God and was created for us to enjoy. But because each of us is unique, the things we enjoy are unique. Some of us

love the mountains and don't care to have sand on/in every part of us to spend the day on a beach. Some of us enjoy whitewater rafting down a river while others would rather hike to a secluded spot and listen to the sound of the wind moving through the trees. The one true thing is that God had each one of us in mind when He created this beautiful earth. He knows us personally, loves us unconditionally, and delights in our joy.

The one thing we should *always* enjoy seeing good in is each other. That's what love does, and that's what God *is*. He's very patient and kind. He isn't easily angered or irritable. He doesn't hold our wrongs against. He's truth and justice. He's faithful to us, no matter what. He sees the best in us and wants the best *for* us. God is good all the time, and loving people the way He does brings out all the good in them. We aren't here to judge, criticize, or change anyone. We're here to love each other more because we love our Creator *most*.

FATHER, FILL ME WITH YOUR LOVE AND LIGHT,
GIVE ME PATIENCE AND GENTLENESS,
AND SHOW ME THE JOY IN SHOWING
YOUR HEART TO OTHERS TODAY.

169

God is always seeking you. Every sunset, every clear blue sky, every ocean wave, the starry host of the night. He blankets each day with the invitation, "I am here."

—LOUIE GIGLIO

IN THE WORDS
OF OUR CAPTAIN

Jesus responded,
"Why are you afraid?
You have so little faith!" Then
He got up and rebuked the wind
and the waves, and suddenly
there was a great calm.

MATTHEW 8:26 NLT

My grandson Troy and I have September birthdays. We share some personality traits too. He has always loved words, people, and staying active. The one thing we don't share is a love of water. I love *looking* at the ocean, but he loves *getting in*. I joke that I have 763 reasons why I don't venture into the ocean when I'm at the beach, and number one is that I've never been a great swimmer. I had a friend who wanted me to travel with him to visit some friends of his who lived on an island. It would take a few hours to get there. I told him I didn't like the idea of being out on the open ocean for that long because my swimming skills were lacking. He said, "If you have a good captain, you don't have to worry about swimming."

We have a good Captain guiding our lives. He's better than any earthly captain because even the wind and the waves obey Him. We don't have to worry about anything. *Ever*. But we do because the cares of this world close in on us. We get overwhelmed with work stress, responsibilities at home, and making sure our people feel loved and cared for. We give until we're worn out, then lay down and worry about more things until we're too tired to sleep. It's a vicious cycle and not an easy one to break.

Our Captain waits patiently for us to ask Him to resume His place at the helm. He'll let us do the steering as long as we choose to, but we might end up far from where we want to be, or worse, farther away from where He wants to take us. We trust Jesus with our eternal destination, why is it hard for us to trust Him with our earthly ones? His direction is clear. *Don't be afraid, follow Me, and love God with all your heart.* Grab hold of grace for today and don't worry, He's already navigated your tomorrow.

FATHER, I GIVE YOU THE CARES OF MY HEART
AND TRUST YOU TO TAKE THE LEAD
IN EVERY AREA OF MY LIFE.

HAPPY ARE THOSE WHO KNOW HIS JOY

Happy are those who hear
the joyful call to worship,
for they will walk in the light
of Your presence, Lord.

PSALM 89:15 NLT

I know our joy doesn't depend on feelings or circumstances or stuff or achievements. And I know that choosing joy is different than being happy—but I *like* being a happy person. I love to smile, and I love seeing how faces change in response to a big, bright, smile. I think hearts can discern an everyday smile from an "I'm in love with Jesus" smile. And I believe it's our deep-seated joy in Him that gives us away!

I once witnessed joy in a dog unlike any joy I've ever seen. It made me so happy! Beachgoing dogs are hands-down one of my favorite things to begin with, but this little Boston Terrier was exceptional. Not only was he trained and

impressively obedient, this little guy loved the ocean. He ran into the water full speed to fetch his toy, but it's what he did when he came out that made me belly laugh. While standing at the water's edge, his owner kicked water into the air, and he started jumping. With a flick of her wrist, the dog jumped straight into the air and did a complete aerial backflip. Over and over again. That was one happy dog making a lot of people on the beach feel happy. If only for a little space of time our hearts felt lighter and we all forgot about any of the heavy things in our lives.

The world could use more joy expressed in happiness these days. We don't have to walk around doing aerial backflips, but we can do a lot of other things. Stay positive. Be courteous. Slow down. Hold doors. Wait our turn. Smile like we know the source of unspeakable, glorious joy. The joy that draws hearts to love. The love that came to save lives. The truest reason to nurture a thankful heart, be contagiously happy, and exude a hope that can't be stopped.

FATHER, MAKE MY HEART HAPPY AT THE THOUGHT
OF YOU AND THE WORLD-CHANGING LOVE
YOU EXPRESS THROUGH MY ACTIONS AND MY LIFE.
SHOW ME NEW WAYS TO BE YOUR JOY.

BREATHING EASY
IN GOD'S CARE

Let us lay aside every weight,
and the sin which so easily
ensnares us, and let us run
with endurance the race
that is set before us.

HEBREWS 12:1 NKJV

All I have to do is think about my first attempt at running on the beach and I feel like I have to stop and catch my breath. It can't be compared to treadmill, trail, or street running. For me, it was difficult and hard to enjoy. I decided quickly I was more of a beach walk girl. I see runners on the beach all the time and they make it look easy. And inspiring. And enjoyable. When people watch the way we live our lives, serving God should look a lot like that. Inspiring, joyful, and filled with a sense of ease knowing we don't have to worry, fear, or give up hope. Our countenance should never look like mine probably did during that first (and last) run on the beach—stressed, strained, and struggling to breathe.

We have the beautiful freedom to breathe easy in God's care. We should live with the same confidence David had when he prayed, "Show Your marvelous lovingkindness by Your right hand, O You who save those who trust in You" (PSALM 17:7 NKJV). We aren't going to collapse on the course God has us running, no matter how impossible it looks or feels. His right hand signifies strength and help whenever we need it, *however* we need it. We trust, He saves. It sounds like we have the much easier task, but so many times we talk ourselves out of trusting, slide into our self-sufficient shoes, and head out the door.

What we see in the natural can persuade us to give up trusting in God's supernatural power to save us. But in the faith race seeing is not believing. Believing God won't fail is how we see our way through, and in time, how we see clearly that He was working things out all along.

FATHER, I REST IN THE STRENGTH
OF YOUR RIGHT HAND AND
TRUST YOU TO MOVE EVERYTHING
INTO PLACE AS I SERVE YOU WITH
A FEARLESS AND HOPEFUL HEART.

ARE WE LOOKING?

Praise Him under the open skies;
praise Him for His acts
of power, praise Him for
His magnificent greatness.

PSALM 150:1-2 THE MESSAGE

Have you ever rode a bicycle on the beach early in the morning? You get to see a lot more of the shoreline than you would on a walk, and the salty air comes at you faster, filling your lungs and fixing a smile on your face. It's like getting a big gulp of God's goodness surrounded by the magnificent greatness of His creation. It so refreshing!

Spending time outdoors can set off a chorus of internal praise. It sometimes feels like your heart is actually swelling from the beauty of it all. And before you know it, you're overwhelmed with gratitude. To think, He made all of this because He loves us and wants us to feel this way. He designed the earth to encourage our hearts to *see* Him in His creation—starry skies, pink sunsets, and aqua-blue waters all reflect His eternal power. If we're having a down day, nature is a good

place to get a pick-me-up. I think that's why children love to be outside. Their spirits, so in tune with God, are energized by the presence of God in everything they see. His divine nature is clearly seen in all that He made. Are we looking for His love in the light of a sunrise, His peace in the quiet stream, or His power in the crash of the ocean waves? It's all there waiting for us to notice.

Our hearts aren't getting much of a break these days. So many things in the world are changing our lives so rapidly, and not all of them in a good way. But God is the same yesterday, today, and forever. His infallible, unchanging Word is the one thing we can hold on to for the hope we need. It's a good time to get outside more often and be reminded that every part of this created earth is a love song written for us by our Father, calling our hearts to praise—praise that He inhabits *joyfully*.

FATHER, THANK YOU FOR
THE BEAUTY OF CREATION AND
THE POWER OF YOUR PRESENCE IN IT.

GROWING
A BIGGER HEART

*Where your treasure is,
there your heart will be also.*

MATTHEW 6:21 NKJV

Of all the achievements, first place finishes, number one rankings, or success we might experience in a lifetime, wouldn't the world be better off if we all aspired to have bigger hearts that spread more love? Did you hear the story about the elementary teacher who passed away unexpectedly? One of the things her students were asked to do to work through their grief was draw a picture of something they thought about when they remembered her. One little boy turned in the sheet of paper he was given, having colored it completely red. When the counselor asked him why he chose to do that he replied, "I tried to draw a picture of her heart, but it was too big for the paper."

Splashing God's love around is worth every minute we spend and every sacrifice we make. What we think are small gestures of kindness can actually become someone's memory of God's great love. Little things make a big impact. Especially if they come from the overflow of a heart in love with God. We don't get the credit for loving other people because we wouldn't be good at it if we didn't know God. He's the hope, the courage, the strength, the patience, the grace, the kindness, and the goodness we give because perfect love is who He is. We have all the supply we'll ever need; we just have to draw from the well and pour it out.

God's love is where we go for the pure, powerful stuff that changes lives, starting with our own. His love is an unbreakable lifeline to the world and we're the ones He's counting on to throw it out there. He'll lead us to the hearts drowning in hopelessness and fear. The hearts needing tenderness and care. We just have to stay close to Him and be willing to be like Jesus.

FATHER, THERE ARE SO MANY WAYS
TO SHOW YOUR LOVE TO THOSE
WHO ARE HURTING AND SEARCHING FOR IT.
HELP ME BE SENSITIVE TO THE NEEDS
AROUND ME TODAY.

COVERED COMPLETELY BY GOD'S GRACE

How happy you must be —
you get a fresh start,
your slate's wiped clean.

PSALM 32:1 THE MESSAGE

Happy is what we *should* be every morning when we open our eyes and God hands us a fresh start and a clean slate. His grace might seem oceanic, but it's so much bigger than that! Water covers about 71 percent of the earth and the oceans make up 96.5 percent of it. Grace covers *100 percent* of our sin for *100 percent* of our lives. God gathered together the waters and gave us the beauty of oceans, seas, lakes, and rivers, which we're thankful for every time we see and enjoy them. But when God graciously offered the life of His Son to take our sin and give us the beauty of a new life, we got something to be *eternally* grateful for.

It's easy to get caught up in mental reruns of yesterday when we mess up and do things we know we shouldn't.

Maybe we lost our temper and damaged a relationship or did something we know God isn't pleased with. If we ask for forgiveness, we're the only ones watching the replay. God wiped the slate clean as soon as we repented. And if we do our part to mend a relationship by apologizing to the one we offended, we have to trust the rest of the healing to God. I spent some time in a rut a few years ago, when I was doing everything God told me to do to repair a close relationship. My efforts proved fruitless, so I put it down and kept praying. God is *so* faithful, and His grace is always sufficient. He restored the relationship and changed both of our hearts in the process. It's back to beautiful because of *Him*.

We can enjoy rest instead of inviting stress if we make a habit of leaning into God's love for us. "God showed how much He loved us by sending His one and only Son into the world so that we might have eternal life through Him" (1 JOHN 4:9 NLT). Look up and lean in today, you're loved lavishly and covered in grace—and there's a fresh start with your name on it.

FATHER, I'M REFRESHED BY YOUR LOVE
AND THE GIFT OF GRACE.

THINK, THINK, THINK
WHAT IS
TRUE, TRUE, TRUE

Be angry, and do not sin.
Meditate within your heart...
and be still.

PSALM 4:4 NKJV

I "meditate within my heart" a lot while I'm sitting on the beach. Being still, taking some time alone, and thinking before responding are the points of wisdom given in this Psalm. And they're good ones. I've shed a lot of tears while sitting still and staring at the ocean, some during sweet times of praise, some when I'm thankful and thinking about what God is doing in my life, and some when my heart is surrendering things to Him that are hard to let go of. If we spend time being still, praying, and getting to a quiet place to listen, we usually know what we need to do. For me, God's direction comes in thoughts, and I recognize them by the gentleness and love that carry them.

God doesn't guide us by making us feel defeated, or by planting thoughts that steal our hope and destroy our self-image. We're created in His image and it's a beautiful one. We only have to go to His Word to know how He feels about us—"I've never quit loving you and I never will. Expect love, love, and more love!" (JEREMIAH 31:3 THE MESSAGE). We're in His thoughts constantly and He wants us to think about His *truth* constantly. His Word dispels every lie that comes into our head. Not one false narrative can stand against the truth of what God says about us. And there's absolutely *nothing* that can separate us from His love.

Our heart can enjoy *rest*, our soul can *relax*, and our mind can have *peace* knowing we have a Father who loves us too much to want anything but the best for our lives. When we spend some time being still enough to *listen*, let's make sure we're hearing and believing the things that make us feel loved, brave, hopeful, and encouraged—anything other than that isn't coming from our Father.

FATHER, GIVE ME THE WISDOM
TO CAST DOWN EVERY THOUGHT THAT ISN'T
IN AGREEMENT WITH THE TRUTH OF
YOUR WORD AND YOUR UNFAILING LOVE.

THE GREATEST LIGHT
BEARERS OF ALL

Praise Him who planted
the water within the earth,
for His lovingkindness
continues forever.

PSALM 136:6 TLB

*G*od's *lovingkindness*. Poured into the oceans and carved into the mountains. Sprinkled in fields of wildflowers and rolled into every wave that reaches the shore. Painted into skies of blue and scattered over the darkness in billions of stars. The definition of lovingkindness is *tenderness and consideration toward others*. Everything God created is for the purpose of revealing His tenderness and consideration toward us. How different would the world be if we made lovingkindness our goal? If we filtered everything we do through the questions, "Does this look like tenderness? Is this considerate of others?" It sounds like a lot of looking past ourselves and investing in

everyone around us. God has given us all of creation to see it clearly.

There was an orca whale known to researchers as J35, who swam with her dead calf for 17 days in an apparent act of grieving. In 2018, the whale who's been named Tahlequah, swam about 1,000 miles of ocean with the body of her dead calf. The calf had died a few hours after birth, but the mother prevented it from sinking for more than two weeks. Could her actions have been more loving or tender? Everything God created is part of who He is and every part of creation is a beautiful reflection of His love. Because we're created in His image, we should be the greatest light bearers of all. We should be careful with one another. We should consider the effect our words and actions will have on those around us before we follow through with them.

Loving God with our whole heart means loving when it's hard to do, being kind when our patience is gone, showing tenderness in a tough situation, and putting others first when it's the last thing we feel they deserve. Kindness makes a way for God's love to have its way in the hearts that need it *most*. And turning a heart toward God is a chance we should never turn down.

FATHER, LET YOUR LOVINGKINDNESS COME
THROUGH IN EVERYTHING I SAY AND DO TODAY.
HELP ME BE ALL THAT LOVE SHOULD BE.

The things we see
don't last. But the things
we do from a gentle,
quiet spirit that's
submitted to God
last forever.

—BONNIE RICKNER JENSEN

AWESOME LOVE IN EVERY LITTLE THING

You answer us with awesome and righteous deeds, God our Savior, the hope of all the ends of the earth and of the farthest seas.

PSALM 65:5 NIV

Is your hope strong today? God is thinking about you and lining up some ways to show how much He loves you. It's okay to let go of the things you were worrying about last night and get excited about seeing how God is going to take care of *every single one of them*. He's going to answer your heart's cry, be sure of it. God answers even when we don't ask. He steps in with strength to shore up our weaknesses because He'll never leave us alone. We're going to get through because *God is who He says He is*.

If we sat down to make a list of the things He's done for us this week, what would it look like? Would seven sunrises and sunsets make the cut? Those are pretty awesome answers to the question, *"Is God faithful?"* Would every moment He gives us to love the people in our lives be noted? Those are amazing answers to the question, *"Is God good?"* Would a home, a good friend, a kind neighbor, health, peace, strength, and joy be written down? Those are comforting answers to the question, *"Does God meet my needs?"* Jesus did what He did so we can be sure the Father will do what He says. And *everything* He does is driven by love.

Next time you start to feel the darkness of the world closing in a little, try to remember the last thing God did to make you smile. No good thing in our lives is accidental, no matter how small. God's love is in all of them. My dad and mom went to heaven last year, three months apart. Since then, I've noticed a pair of cardinals at the feeder outside my window. I giggle as I watch the female sit on the fence while the male cardinal picks up dinner and feeds it to her. Dad waited on Mom quite a bit toward the end and did it so lovingly. Watch closely. Light will come to make you smile, and Love will be the One sending it.

FATHER, YOUR LOVE SURROUNDS ME
AND YOUR HOPE CARRIES ME.
MY HEART IS INCREDIBLY THANKFUL.

QUIETLY HOPING FOR THE TURNAROUND

It's a good thing to quietly hope,
quietly hope for help from God.

LAMENTATIONS 3:26 THE MESSAGE

On a family vacation to Maine we decided to go on a whale watch tour early one morning. As we sailed past the small islands along the coast and made our way into open waters, the fog started to thicken. The captain chose to keep going, telling us the fog would likely lift during the scheduled time set for the outing. We reached the stopping point and it felt like the fog closed in on us. There was about five feet of water visible from the boat and we had to stand at the railing on the deck to see it. By this time, our middle daughter was becoming terribly seasick. She tried to stand with us and look for whales, but the only thing any of us could see were the ocean swells just before they got to the boat. After a short time of looking down—swell, dip, rock, repeat— everyone on the boat was feeling less well, and less in the mood to stick it out. I could tell we were all quietly hoping the captain would

take us back to shore. After a short time of looking at a boat full of longing faces, he decided to return to the dock and give everyone a refund.

How many times in our lives have we made a decision that didn't turn out the way we planned? We get to a point and start quietly hoping for God to intervene and help us get back to a good place. We should *always* quietly hope. It's a good thing to do, and it's a good thing we serve a God who will *always* help us. The turnaround might not happen as fast as we'd like it to, but it will come. He'll make the crooked places straight, the rough places smooth, and His glory will shine in the rescue.

When things go wrong it can lead our hearts to the right place. We spend a lot more time with our Father. Our trust is challenged and when it is, it goes deeper. We learn to quietly hope, every day, until God turns the boat around and gets us back to our peaceful refuge in Him.

FATHER, I TRUST YOUR FAITHFULNESS
AND KNOW MY LIFE IS IN YOUR HANDS.

LITTLE DROPS OF LIGHT FOR ALL TO SEE

I am the Light of the world.
So if you follow Me,
you won't be stumbling through
the darkness, for living light
will flood your path.

JOHN 8:12 TLB

Have you ever noticed the variations of blue and green as you look out over the ocean? It's a different shade almost every time you take a look, right? The brighter the sun, the lighter the water looks. In full sun it waves in a gorgeous palette of turquoise, teal, and aquamarine. When the sun is filtered, the water looks blue. And when the sun is blocked by clouds it looks dark and more gray than blue. There are so many contributing factors to the water color we see, but from a purely non-scientific, beachgoer observation, the amount of sunlight affects it noticeably.

Light matters in our lives too. The closer we are to Jesus the brighter His light becomes in us, and the more beautiful effect we have on those around us. Jesus had a way of touching the hearts of people while making the Father's love the catalyst of change. We should want to do the same. Love speaks to a person's heart more than anything else can or will. It's the brightest light we have to shine in a dark world. Jesus cheered us on when He said, "Don't hide your light! Let it shine for all; let your good deeds glow for all to see, so that they will praise your heavenly Father" (MATTHEW 5:15-16 TLB).

When our path is flooded with the living light of a loving God, we want there to be a lot of good deeds glowing for all to see. The love we show, the kindnesses we do, the joy we spread, the hope we carry—they're like little drops of light leading hearts to the heavenly Father. Nothing we do matters as much, and sharing His love never mattered more.

FATHER, FILL MY DEEDS WITH YOUR LOVE.
LET THE LIGHT OF ETERNITY BE IN THEM
SO EVERY HEART TOUCHED WILL SEE
THE BEAUTY OF YOU.

BEFORE OUR FEET
HIT THE FLOOR

*He set the limits of the seas
and gave them His instructions
not to spread beyond
their boundaries....
He made the blueprint for
the earth and oceans.*

PROVERBS 8:28-29 TLB

When God made the blueprint for the earth, our lives were already sketched into it. "Even before He made the world, God chose us to be His very own through what Christ would do for us" (EPHESIANS 1:4 TLB). Imagine! Our Father knew every one of us before the beginning of time and the creation of earth. He planned the day we'd arrive, had decided on the design for every detail of who we'd be, and then He *chose*

us to be His. Wow. How do we let ourselves spend a minute of our lives worrying about whether or not God understands what we're going through? Or how we let our minds wonder if He sees time is running out for the money we need to pay the mortgage? He saw our lives in whole before we took our first breath—He understands, He sees, and He *knows*.

We're the ones who lose sight of His promises. He never does. He knows them all by heart because they came from His heart and the eternal love that's in it. We lose our focus when we do too much looking around and not enough looking up. We see the circumstances and the mounting obstacles and get ourselves into a panic. We look into all the ways we can scramble to make things work out instead of looking into the promises He's given. Promises we can *always* put our trust in.

God wants to guide us and we want to *let* Him, but stressing out doesn't gel with being still. That doesn't mean we start sitting on our hands, it means we wake up every day and surrender every moment to Him before our feet hit the floor. His plan is already in place—through a friend, an unexpected blessing, or even a stranger—to meet *all* our needs by His riches in glory through the gift of Jesus. God set the limits of the seas and keeps them in place. *He's more than able to keep His promises to us too.*

FATHER, YOUR WORD IS SURE,
AND YOUR LOVE SURROUNDS ME.
ALL OF MY HOPE IS IN YOU.

PEACE, PEACE, WONDERFUL PEACE

*All who humble themselves
before the Lord shall
be given every blessing and
shall have wonderful peace.*

PSALM 37:11 TLB

The peace God gives our heart, mind, and soul isn't the same as the world's definition of peace and quiet. The beach is a noisy place, so what makes us more at peace there than anywhere else on earth? The sound of the waves is constant, at times crashing, and they still bring a calmness. They're a wonderful reminder of the rhythm of grace and God's unfailing love. The seagulls squawk and squeal repeatedly, but their enthusiasm is a joyous reminder that every living, breathing creature is called to praise the Lord (PSALM 150). There are sounds of laughter, children playing, music, and the steady hum of the ocean breeze. All of which are reminders of the

One who created such a beautiful, relaxing, rejuvenating place for us to enjoy.

The physical benefits of ocean air are a bonus to the spiritual rest we get from simply *being* at the beach. If only annual beach vacations were mandated by ruling governments, the whole world would be a happier place! God knows best what we need most, and peaceful hearts and physical rest are both on the list. We can't go, go, go every day without a break and expect every part of us to stay healthy. Our spiritual well-being often gets put aside too easily, because our physical demands are hard to ignore. They press relentlessly on our energy and time. If not kept in check, we can allow daily demands to steal our spiritual strength.

We need to give ourselves time to cultivate a quiet spirit. Whether it be at a beach, on a walk around the block, relaxing in the back yard, or cozied up on the couch. Geography doesn't matter, spending time with God does. His peace is a blessing worth settling into as often as we can, for whatever space of time we can, for rest our hearts can *always* use.

FATHER, PEACE OF HEART AND MIND
IS A GIFT OF YOUR UNFAILING LOVE AND
AMAZING GRACE. SHOW ME WAYS I CAN
MAKE IT A PRIORITY IN MY DAY.

BECOMING

*Be beautiful inside,
in your hearts, with the lasting
charm of a gentle and quiet
spirit that is so precious to God.*

I PETER 3:4 TLB

We are all self-conscious about beach attire and how we look in it, and it's easy to wrap yourself in a big beach blanket of insecurity. Even though I know truth tells us *not* to make outward beauty our main concern, it's easy to forget in a world where everything from advertising to social media puts the focus on our appearance. Now we have hundreds of filters that let us feed the false sense of security we get from looking perfect on the outside. We can fall prey to the notion that our value is based on our looks, and we have to be adamant about telling ourselves the truth. God puts the highest value on what our *heart* looks like, not on the profile pics we post.

The things we see don't last. But the things we do from a gentle, quiet spirit that's submitted to God last *forever*. Things like loving everyone in our lives and staying thankful

about *having* people to love. Things like opening our lives to opportunities that allow us to lovingly serve people we don't know but know could use our help. Things like small kindnesses and big smiles when the Holy Spirit gives our heart a nudge, knowing it'll make all the difference in someone's day. It might even move their heart to look at their heavenly Father, who's been looking for ways to bring them back into His arms.

We are all guilty of getting things out of order every once in a while, blending the truth with the lie, using filters to erase my wrinkles, and checking too often for the number of likes. When we focus on such things, we are wasting the time God has given us on keeping the superficial need for approval alive, which is never a good thing. But this is a journey of growing wiser in truth, getting closer to God, and giving our gentle, quiet spirits time to *become*. We'll keep at it together and give each other grace along the way. And by the way, you look *beautiful* today.

FATHER, TURN MY HEART AND MY EYES
TO THE TRUTH THAT MY TRUE BEAUTY COMES
FROM YOU. MAKE MY HEART HOME
TO YOUR GENTLE, COMPASSIONATE LOVE
MORE AND MORE EVERY DAY.

ONE-ON-ONE WITH OUR FATHER

I will quietly keep my mind upon Your promises.

PSALM 119:95 TLB

It's good to be quietly hopeful, good to be quietly prayerful, and good to quietly keep our minds on every promise God has given to us. A phrase many used when tempted to get too many people involved in something is: *confidence is silent, insecurities are loud.* Faith is confident hope. Our security is in Jesus. And sometimes, God wants us to rest quietly in the assurance He's planted in our hearts and trust Him to hold us without any other hearts or hands involved. Simply put, He enjoys a little one-on-one faith building now and then.

Do you have a few good friends who are fervent intercessors that you can open up to about a lot of what's going on in your life and the things you're trusting God for? There are certainly many times when our hearts need support and encouragement from the body of Christ, and times God wants us to gather together and get in agreement when we fight spiritual battles.

But He's a loving Father too and likes us to remember we can approach Him quietly and confidently any time of any day.

One of my best friends is a pastor's wife and a prayer warrior. She told me a story of being a young married couple, having very little, and one night craving a pizza they couldn't afford. She didn't voice her desire but kept it quietly to herself. Someone from their church decided to bless them with dinner that night, and they chose to have pizza delivered. Those are small gestures to remind us that nothing in our lives is insignificant when it comes to the care of our heavenly Father. He sees everything and loves to let us know He's watching. Love feels true and sweet when we know that we're *known*—and God knows us better than anyone on this earth ever will.

FATHER, THANK YOU FOR PAYING CLOSE ATTENTION TO MY NEEDS AND REMINDING ME THAT NOTHING IN MY LIFE IS TOO SMALL FOR YOUR LOVING CARE.

OUR LIFE'S LIGHTHOUSE

He is my Savior,
a rock where none can reach me,
and a tower of safety.

PSALM 18:2 TLB

Don't you just love lighthouses? They're towers built to be beacons guiding boats in and out of safe harbor or warning them of dangerous shallows and rocky coasts. We have a *built-in* light and navigator keeping us safe and guiding us through life. God gave us Jesus to be the tower of safety He knew we would need. Without Him we'd be lost and unequipped to make it through the storms, dangers, and darkness of this world—and God wasn't about to let it happen. He loved us too much to leave us stranded. He built us an eternal lighthouse through the life and death of His son, and it's a place we can look to for redemption and go to for refuge.

Whenever we feel the waters of life rising and the waves

overtaking the strength of our heart or the peace in our soul, we have a light in our spirit to lead us safely through. Jesus has been where we are, felt what we're going through, and come out with *everything* we'll ever need in His hand. Nothing we face can overcome His all-sufficient grace. Jesus put all we need for an abundant life in the win column. All we have to do is remind ourselves, of the final tally. There aren't any losses when we spend our lives serving God. Love is a win. Hope never loses. Trust brings victory every single time.

By learning to rest in the refuge of Jesus, we learn what it means to truly live. We stop striving and start seeking His guidance every day. We stop flailing in the darkness and start focusing on the light leading us to safety. We stop testing the waters of self-dependence and start stretching our faith in the God we serve. He's not going to let us down. He's going to keep pulling us up and setting our feet on the Rock—where nothing can reach us and love *always* redeems us.

FATHER, YOU ARE MY TOWER OF SAFETY
AND THE ONE I TRUST TO LEAD ME THROUGH
EVERY STORM I FACE IN THIS LIFE.

THE POWER TO REFRESH IN THE WORDS WE CHOOSE

What joy! May we be refreshed as by streams in the desert.

PSALM 126:3-4 TLB

Have you ever noticed all the people who read at the beach? Sitting comfortably under a colorful umbrella, they quietly enjoy a well-written story or a book filled with words of motivation, information, or revelation. Words are powerful. They can lift us out of a sad place or take us to one. They can encourage us to be better or they can discourage us from trying. God has given us the best life manual, the greatest love story, and the most encouraging words we'll ever find in *one* book. If our hearts need real refreshing, God's Word is where we go.

It's a lot easier to choose the words we read than it is to control the words we speak. They can come out too quickly and with too little thought when we're angry. They can be contrary to what God says about us when we feel insecure. They can be disrespectful when we gossip, and they can be critical when we forget God has called us to love people, not to judge them. Proverbs 16:24 says, "Kind words are like honey—enjoyable and healthful." Words affect health, both ours and the people who hear them. One translation says that pleasant words sweeten the soul and give health to our bones. Spoken words have a deep and lasting effect. They can be life-giving or they can make life harder to live, and isn't it hard enough already?

What would happen if we all chose words that are as *refreshing* as streams in the desert. Words that fill souls with joy and hearts with hope. By taking every opportunity to speak a kind word, give a compliment, say something positive, or let someone know they're loved, we change our little corner of the world *today*. And if we keep speaking words of life day-after-day, we keep changing lives one-by-one. We need each other more than ever right now, to be light bringers and love spreaders, hope holders and courage builders, kind doers and strength givers. God has *all* the word power we'll ever need—we just need to be the ones speaking it.

FATHER, FILL MY HEART WITH LOVE
AND KINDNESS SO THE WORDS I SPEAK REVEAL
THE LIFE YOU GIVE.

LIVE YOUR FAITH

Dear Friend,

This book was prayerfully crafted with you, the reader, in mind. Every word, every sentence, every page was thoughtfully written, designed, and packaged to encourage you—right where you are this very moment. At DaySpring, our vision is to see every person experience the life-changing message of God's love. So, as we worked through rough drafts, design changes, edits, and details, we prayed for you to deeply experience His unfailing love, indescribable peace, and pure joy. It is our sincere hope that through these Truth-filled pages your heart will be blessed, knowing that God cares about you—your desires and disappointments, your challenges and dreams.

He knows. He cares. He loves you unconditionally.

BLESSINGS!
THE DAYSPRING BOOK TEAM

Additional copies of this book and
other DaySpring titles can be purchased
at fine retailers everywhere.
Order online at <u>dayspring.com</u>
or
by phone at 1-877-751-4347

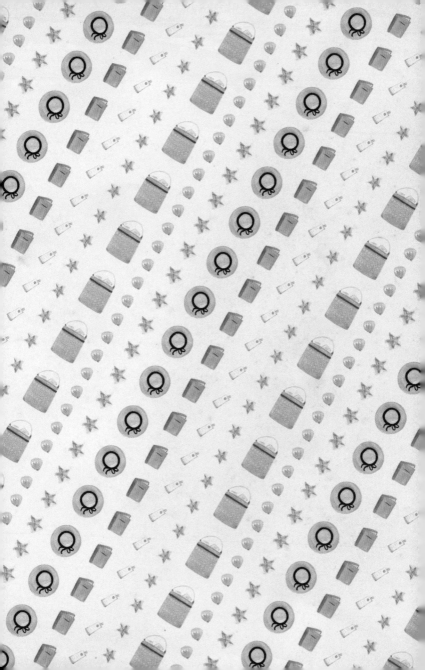

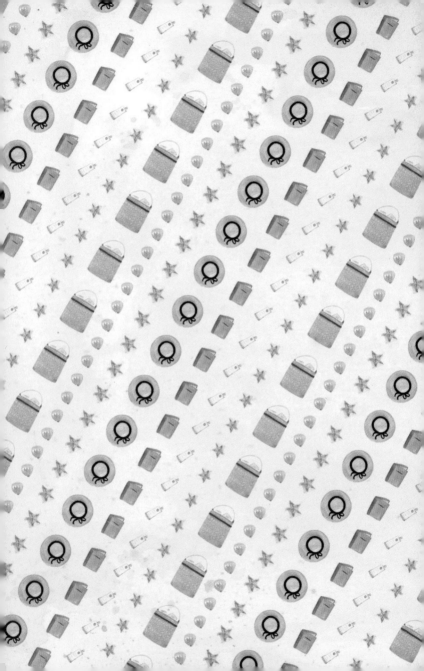